MW00637027

QUALITY MAINTENANCE

QUALITY MAINTENANCE

ZERO DEFECTS THROUGH
EQUIPMENT MANAGEMENT

Seiji Tsuchiya

Productivity Press
Portland, Oregon

Originally published as *MQM ni yoru hinshitsu huryō zero e no chōsen*, copyright ©1991 by Japan Management Association, Tokyo.

English edition copyright © 1992 by Productivity Press, a division of Productivity, Inc. Translated by John Loftus.

All rights reserved. No part of this book may be reproduced or utilized in any form or by any means, electronic or mechanical, including photocopying, recording, or by any information storage and retrieval system, without permission in writing from the publisher. Additional copies of this book are available from the publisher. Discounts are available for multiple copies through the Sales Department (800-394-6868). Address all other inquiries to:

Productivity Press
P.O. Box 13390
Portland, OR   97213-0390
United States of America
Telephone: 503-235-0600
Telefax: 503-235-0909
E-mail: service@ppress.com

Cover design by Gary Ragaglia
Printed by Advanced Digital Imaging, Inc., Portland, Oregon
Printed in the United States of America

Library of Congress Cataloging-in-Publication Data

Tsuchiya, Seiji.
 [MQM ni yoru hinshitsu huryō zero e no chōsen. English]
 Quality maintenance: zero defects through equipment management /
Seiji Tsuchiya.
  p. cm.
 Translation of: MQM ni yoru hinshitsu huryō zero e no chōsen.
 Includes index.
 ISBN 0-56327-137-0
 1. Industrial equipment--Maintenance and repair--Management.
2. Production management--Quality control. 3. Just-in-time systems.
I. Title.
TS191.T88 1992
658.5′6--dc20   91-44043
                                                                        CIP
                                                                        rev.

First paperback edition 1996

02 01 00 99 98 97   10 9 8 7 6 5 4 3 2

Contents

Publisher's Message

More and more American companies are entering the race to implement TPM. The most successful competitors, however, are reaping the benefits of the kind of shop-floor empowerment and cooperative management reflected in this case study of a quality-focused equipment management program.

In developing a TPM strategy at Furukawa Electric, author Seiji Tsuchiya adhered to two guiding principles:

- The best improvements should cost the least relative to their impact.
- These improvements are best achieved through managerial and educational improvements that involve everyone.

Team-based strategies like shop-floor work standardization and control (Five S) and autonomous quality maintenance by operators will yield greater long-term results than staff-implemented hardware improvements standing alone. Hardware solutions, observes Tsuchiya, are often incomplete — they do not address all factors contributing to chronic problems; they also tend to be corrective rather than preventive in nature.

"Software" (managerial) solutions, on the other hand, properly implemented can anticipate and prevent problems before they occur — at a lower cost.

Unfortunately, in many environments many members of the work force are unable to analyze problems or implement improvements effectively. The best long-term strategy, however, is still a team-based program, Tsuchiya argues. When individuals with diverse perspectives and skills come together with concrete improvement objectives and strategies in hand, they can accomplish much in relatively short intervals. Careful planning and management of team activities are the keys.

An excellent example is Furukawa Electric's deployment of equipment improvement activities, detailed in Chapter 6. Cross-functional and cross-divisional improvement teams meet in carefully planned one-day whirlwind sessions to address specific problems; these sessions inspire enthusiasm in local areas to follow up and maintain the improvements implemented. Regular events like these afford continuous opportunities to share knowledge, learn new team skills, and discover the advantages of thorough research and planning.

The Five S and autonomous quality maintenance activities for operators described in Chapter 3 are equally well planned and orchestrated. These activities carried out in tandem with equipment improvements yielded excellent results for Furukawa Electric in terms of quality improvement as well as a more flexible, skilled, and motivated work force at every level of the organization.

In environments where shop-floor diagnostic and improvement skills are not nurtured in this way, operators end up like automatons, maintenance personnel as mere handymen, and equipment problems are addressed only by specialized staff — people who are highly skilled, but not involved in operating or managing the equipment on a daily basis. In such an environment the connections between defective outputs, equipment conditions, and equipment management can never be fully understood.

Understanding and controlling these connections is, in fact, the goal of quality maintenance, or MQP management as it is called at Furukawa Electric. A shop-floor quality maintenance program goes beyond equipment improvement and traditional autonomous maintenance activities. "The aim of MQP management is to achieve perfect quality assurance by identifying and thoroughly controlling the relationship between product quality and the deterioration of both processing conditions and equipment parts." This involves a rigorous program of shop-floor education and carefully designed and managed standardization and control activities. Carried out over the complete life of equipment, it applies to every mechanism that can have an impact on quality, including dies and molds, fixtures and tools, quality inspection equipment, and testing devices and measuring instruments. Other Productivity books related to TPM have introduced the rigorous improvement methodology known as P-M analysis, which supports the TPM pillar of equipment improvement activity. This book offers the next step — MQP analysis or quality maintenance — a highly detailed, step-by-step enhancement of the traditional TPM approach to eliminating chronic loss.

Two guiding principles of quality maintenance are worth noting: preemptive control (eliminating or controlling the sources of defects) and visual control (making abnormalities easy to discern and correct and facilitating the monitoring of large numbers of factors). An important prerequisite to preemptive control is solid understanding of equipment conditions and the mechanisms of failures and defects. The enormous amount of data gathering, observation, analysis, and experimentation involved in identifying these "quality components" in equipment can be carried out effectively only through cross-functional teamwork. Moreover, effective control of these components can be achieved only through close cooperation among engineering, maintenance, and production staff. It requires all employees in the company to be willing to change the way they think about and take responsibility for quality — and equipment.

Visual control — along with its foundational activity, workplace standardization or Five S — is absolutely essential in a zero-defects, zero-failures environment. These goals are supported by control activities that go beyond the observations or response of any individual or intelligent system. Everyone on the shop floor must share in the responsibility for preventing abnormal conditions from occurring or producing a quality failure. Visual controls help make this possible by making it easier to *see* a deviation from standards, *understand* what is required, and *carry out* the required corrective action properly. This book features many examples of simple controls that originated and were implemented right on the shop floor.

Furukawa Electric implemented just-in-time (JIT) production after getting its quality maintenance program off the ground. In recommending that companies start with TPM first, Tsuchiya notes what many JIT managers have observed: that JIT requires excellent equipment and quality. He also notes what many Toyota managers confirm: that equipment and quality programs are tested and proven in the fire of JIT; the greater demands of JIT are the real drivers of TPM and quality improvement. His chapter on TPM and JIT is full of sage observations and practical advice on implementing both programs together.

The most impressive feature of this book is its clear direction to management — middle-management in particular — about its role in planning, orchestrating, and supporting the change process. In every chapter, the author balances detailed description of the various improvement activities with plenty of concrete advice and how-to's about the backstage support required of managers. In many respects, this is a manager's handbook on the nuts and bolts of quality maintenance implementation.

We would like to express our appreciation to Seiji Tsuchiya and to Hiroshi Shimizu, director of the publication and information development division of the Japan Management Association, and Kazuya Uchiyama, managing director of the JMA Management Center, for giving us the opportunity to create this English-language edition of their fine book.

Our thanks go to John Loftus for providing an excellent English translation; to Bruce Graham for editorial development (with assistance from Karen Jones); to Dorothy Lohmann for managing the manuscript editing and preparation (with assistance from Laura St. Clair and Peter Tietjen); to Jennifer Cross for the index; to David Lennon and Gayle Joyce for production management; to Caroline Kutil and Karla Tolbert for art preparation and typesetting; and to Gary Ragaglia for the cover design.

Norman Bodek
Chairman, Productivity, Inc.

Connie Dyer
Director of TPM Development, Productivity, Inc.

Foreword to the
Japanese Edition

Seiji Tsuchiya is a born engineer who joined Furukawa Electric in 1956 and has served as engineering department manager at our four production plants in Yokohama, Chiba, Hiratsuka, and Kyūshū. The main job of the engineering department in factories from the mid-1950s to the mid-1960s was repair and maintenance, and this tended to be a thankless task overshadowed by the production function. Maintenance personnel were inclined to think they had nothing to do with product quality or yields and that their only job was to see how fast they could fix broken equipment. But Mr. Tsuchiya realized that high-quality products cannot be made unless every operator in the workplace becomes an expert on his or her equipment and uses it to build quality into the process. For many years, he has stressed that high quality products cannot be made with the "I make it — you fix it" attitude, and has worked hard to bring the company around to this viewpoint. His efforts bore fruit; Furukawa Electric started a companywide TPM (total productive maintenance) campaign in 1977, with Mr. Tsuchiya as team leader, under the guidance of the late Yoshikazu Takahashi of the Institute of Productive Maintenance Technology.

While promoting this campaign, Mr. Tsuchiya made a habit of visiting the factory floor himself to give hands-on guidance, and operators became highly knowledgeable about their own equipment. As a result they acquired the habit of keeping their machines well lubricated and all hardware properly secured; they also began to notice the slightest unusual sounds or temperature increases, immediately reporting them to the engineering department. When repairs were carried out, the operators always watched and helped, and the number of unexpected breakdowns dropped dramatically in every plant. However, Mr. Tsuchiya was not content with this; he took conventional TPM a step further by aiming at the complete elimination of quality defects. As a means of building in quality through equipment, he established and implemented the MQP management system, which clearly defines the relationships among machines (M), quality (Q), and people (P). In this way, he succeeded in radically transforming the very nature of our factories.

This book contains a wealth of specific examples based on the author's experience. Line managers and instructors will certainly find it an exceptionally practical and useful text.

Recently, many companies have attempted to introduce the JIT (just-in-time) system, and Furukawa Electric has also taken up this challenge. In addition to his other responsibilities, Mr. Tsuchiya is division manager of our JIT promotion team. This book clearly describes the position of TPM within the JIT system, and emphasizes that all efforts to make JIT work will fail without a continual striving toward the goal of zero equipment breakdowns. Mr. Tsuchiya has learned this lesson from recent experience, and I believe his remarks are worth careful study, particularly by anyone tackling JIT.

Manabu Asamura
Former Executive Vice President
Furukawa Aluminum Industries Co., Ltd.
(Former Senior Managing Director,
Furukawa Electric Co., Ltd.)

Preface

Plants and equipment are becoming more and more complex and automated, and progress is even being made toward entirely automated factories. This trend, together with the recent increase in the sophistication of quality requirements, has made it essential that quality be built into products through the production process and the equipment itself. One consequence is that maintenance, the basis of all manufacturing activity, has come into the spotlight — particularly maintenance with total employee involvement (total productive maintenance), which has been established and developed in many Japanese companies and is now spreading around the world. It attracts less attention and is less glamorous than other *kaizen** activities, particularly in a plant that is not fully utilized and where spare capacity exists. Nevertheless, maintenance is an indispensable part of manufacturing and is the most basic of all production activities. For this reason, all managers in a company from top executives down to division and department managers must be

---

* *Kaizen* means continuous incremental improvement of the process, work methods, and work site through employee ideas and activities.

clear about its necessity and aims. They must understand it, take an interest in it, and tirelessly promote it.

Every year, factories and offices all over Japan use productive maintenance to achieve excellent results, and companies outside Japan are also achieving success with TPM. It is being used, albeit with some differences in how it is promoted, in all kinds of manufacturing industries as well as in the process and the component industries.

Companywide TPM activities have been evolving at Furukawa Electric for over a decade, since 1977, and are steadily extended to the company's affiliates. TPM formed the basis of Furukawa's "NF-87 Campaign" (a campaign started in 1985 with the aim of reforming the entire corporate culture), and it contributed greatly to the success of the campaign. As one of the promoters of TPM within Furukawa, I am convinced of its tremendous value. This book summarizes my TPM experience with specific examples, focusing particularly on quality. I hope that it will be widely used both for general reading and as a practical manual. Since it seeks to clarify the relation among equipment, quality, and human behavior (machines, quality, and people), the management technique described in this book is known at Furukawa as MQP Management. It is widely recognized as a highly effective means of eradicating process defects.

Many books have been written about TPM, but few contain specific examples of the relation between equipment and quality even though research into this is urgently needed. Furukawa Electric has promoted MQP management as part of its TPM drive because it is a technique that suits the characteristics of manufacturing plants. This book describes my thoughts on MQP management and its promotion, together with specific techniques and case studies derived from my own experience. The final chapter discusses the relation between the JIT production system and TPM, clarifying their mutual roles. I will be happy if this book helps managers and engineers reduce defects and improve the way they manage their factories.

In this book, I have discussed the philosophy and promotion methods behind the ZD challenge, based on my experience. While the demand for even more sophisticated equipment and maintenance technology will keep on growing and research into these areas will continue without pause, I am aware that I lack experience in many aspects of them.

In the future, I would like to devote more effort to pursuing these lines of inquiry, and am eager to learn from my teachers and others more experienced than I. I warmly thank everyone who has read this book and invite their comments and opinions.

I would like to express my sincere appreciation to Dr. Fumio Ishiyama, former senior managing director of Furukawa Electric and now president of Furukawa Industry, for his advice and encouragement.

I would also like to acknowledge the guidance on TPM that I received from the late Mr. Yoshikazu Takahashi as well as from Mr. Takashi Osada, president of the Institute of Productive Maintenance Technology. I received much assistance with the publication of this book from Mr. Kazuya Uchiyama, assistant manager of the Publishing and Information Division Headquarters of the JMA Management Center.

I have also received tremendous support from Mr. Manabu Asamura, former executive vice president of Furukawa Aluminum Industries Co., Ltd. (former senior managing director of the Furukawa Electric Co., Ltd.), who advised me from day to day on various aspects of the activities described here, and many others at Furukawa. Mr. Tetsuro Terada, head of the Production Efficiency Promoting Group, and Mr. Youichi Fukumoto, manager of the Engineering Division, kindly revised the manuscript. I would like to express my sincere gratitude to all of the above.

Seiji Tsuchiya

1

The Zero Defect Challenge

This chapter discusses the background and significance of TPM and one of its techniques, MQP management.* It also explains the importance of the ZD (zero defect) challenge.

QUALITY REQUIREMENTS

As markets grow more diversified and sophisticated, there is a trend toward products with higher added value; and higher levels of product quality are demanded in all areas of industry. Many electric cable and nonferrous metal products are used for applications requiring great reliability, and defects, even on the order of ppm, are impermissible.

For example, cables must have no initial defects along their length and must sustain highly sensitive, low-loss transmission over long distances under adverse environmental conditions. Similarly, electronic products must have no minor defects such

---

* MQP management seeks to clarify the relation between equipment, quality, and human behavior (machines, quality, people).

as surface damage or discoloration even in small samples taken from bulk materials.

QUALITY ASSURANCE

The role of the shop floor in quality assurance is to build quality into the process, so that defects are neither created nor passed on from one operation to the next. As processes become more automated, using equipment to build in quality becomes increasingly important.

In the past, final inspection was the principal check for quality. If it is the *only* effort to prevent defects from being passed on, however, problems arise. In recent years, it has become necessary to conduct inspections at each operation. Furthermore, to achieve zero defects, quality must be built into the entire process. Following are some problems created by relying on final inspection.

- It is often impossible in a final inspection to examine every article in a lot, every centimeter of cable or every characteristic of a product.
- Even if final inspection is performed with utmost care, the procedure itself may be inadequate.
- Using sampling inspection, it is difficult to assure the quality of the entire production run.
- When inspection data is plotted on control charts to reveal trends and to find the causes of defects, it is often impossible to identify the causal relationships or analyze the causes because of the random nature of the defects and the multiplicity of causes.
- Even if defects can be detected during a final inspection, each occurrence can entail a heavy financial loss.

CAUSES OF PROBLEMS

To improve quality and reduce costs, both skilled and unskilled work is being mechanized. More sophisticated, automated and computerized equipment is available and in use. Still, problems persist. Many problems are now due to poor handling and inspection of equipment. An outdated or ineffective equipment maintenance system results in frequent breakdowns. And as quality requirements become more stringent, each failure or defect creates larger losses. Losses also occur if protective devices, gauges, sensors, and measuring instruments are not handled and inspected properly, since these are indispensable to quality assurance.

As mechanization advances, equipment reliability becomes more vital to ensuring quality. Unforeseen, sporadic problems that have not previously occurred pose a worrisome threat and result in serious losses. Every effort must be made to prevent them.

BENEFITS OF ZERO DEFECTS

Coping with the modern demand for high-variety, low-volume, short-lead-time production requires manufacturing in small lots and keeping materials and products moving smoothly through the factory. Lead times must shrink and inventory must be minimized, but without disrupting the process. So it is vital to anticipate and to prevent equipment breakdowns and product defects.

If inventory is eliminated for a process in which each operation employs only one machine, then any equipment breakdown or product defect can halt the entire factory, not just the particular operation involved.

Eliminating defects improves not only quality but also all aspects of production. It has a wide-ranging impact on production capacity, boosting operation rates and line speeds, shortening production cycle times, cutting material losses, saving energy, making workerless operation possible (cost), and slashing inventories and lead times (delivery). It helps enormously to raise the performance level of the entire factory, not only increasing efficiency in generating existing products, but also encouraging the introduction of new products and the use of new equipment.

MQP MANAGEMENT AS AN INTEGRAL PART OF TPM

This section outlines the fundamentals of TPM and MQP management, and describes how they can be implemented.

Definition and Goals of TPM

Total productive maintenance (TPM), or "PM by everybody," was defined in 1971 by the Japan Institute of Plant Engineers (JIPE) (forerunner of the Japan Institute for Plant Maintenance) as follows:

TPM is designed to maximize equipment effectiveness (improving overall efficiency) by establishing a comprehensive productive maintenance system covering the entire life of the equipment, spanning all equipment-related fields (planning, use, maintenance, etc.) and, with the participation of all employees from top management down to shop-floor workers, to promote productive maintenance through "motivation management," or voluntary small-group activities.

TPM is equipment-directed management. As such, it must lay an educational groundwork that trains as many workers as possible in the fundamentals and key components of the equipment they use. It takes a medium to long-term approach, and achieves its results by working with other management activities.

The value of deploying TPM is widely recognized, particularly in today's increasingly mechanized and automated production facilities, yet it is not easy to ensure its implementation at the core of modern, large-scale production processes. Voluntary efforts and equipment improvement can produce astounding results. Still, such results aren't likely to occur overnight. Although it cannot be measured in the short term, the increased level of control achieved through TPM represents a tremendous asset. TPM aims at maintaining the optimal condition of equipment, and upgrading maintenance skills (see Figure 1-1).

In recent years, markets have been shaken up by high-tech products that use advanced technologies to full advantage.

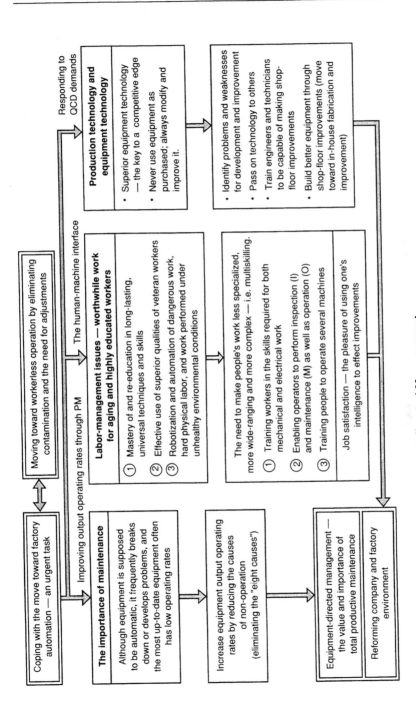

Figure 1-1. The Importance of Equipment-directed Management

These products have appeared not only in consumer markets but also on the shop floor in the form of new production equipment designed to increase productivity and improve quality. This trend underscores the importance of a maintenance system that identifies and maintains the peak condition of such advanced equipment.

TPM uses an *output operating rate* to indicate equipment effectiveness, but these figures are only considered reliable when they are obtained from computer-processed daily work log data (see Figure 1-2).

Still, it's possible to obtain a working output operating rate from the daily work log by tallying the actual output, calculating the theoretical output (the output that would be achieved in the same operating time if products were made at the theoretical

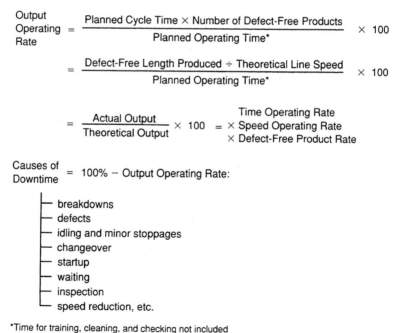

*Time for training, cleaning, and checking not included

**Figure 1-2. Effective Equipment Utilization
(Improving the Output Operating Rate)**

speed without equipment stops), and dividing the former by the latter. This does not have to be done continually; it is sufficient to do it for a specified time.

In other words, you must analyze the factors behind the nonoperation of equipment (represented by 100 percent minus the output operating rate) then attempt to reduce or eliminate them. Remember that, surprisingly enough, new equipment often has a lower output operating rate than older equipment because of the higher incidence of problems, and because it requires more work-hours for corrective action. Obviously, automatic equipment is designed to work without an operator. If the equipment is reliable, fine; if it is not, an operator must monitor it constantly to ensure that no problems occur, thereby defeating the purpose of installing the new equipment. How the promotion of autonomous maintenance results in a dramatic decrease in breakdowns is illustrated in Figure 1-3. However, in this example, the subsequent startup of new equipment and the introduction of new products caused an increase in the number of failures, albeit temporary. This illustrates the great importance of new-equipment maintenance.

TPM also aims at upgrading maintenance skills. If workers become interested and involved in maintenance, they learn the basic principles and key points of their equipment. And as they develop their ability to maintain and improve their equipment, they get a sense of accomplishment and satisfaction.

Industry is moving away from human labor and relying more and more on machines; manufacturing equipment is becoming more sophisticated and automated; elimination of the need for adjustments is removing the need for highly skilled labor. Workers spend more time on simple jobs such as changeovers and become unable to help with improvements even when they try.

Meanwhile, there is the problem of the higher educational levels of young workers and the "graying" of older workers. To cope with this, they all must be equipped with worthwhile skills and techniques that do not quickly become obsolete. Teaching multiple skills and maintenance techniques is one solution to

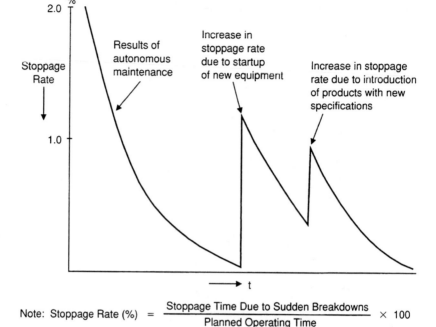

Note: Stoppage Rate (%) = $\dfrac{\text{Stoppage Time Due to Sudden Breakdowns}}{\text{Planned Operating Time}} \times 100$

Figure 1-3. Increase in Breakdowns Due to Introduction of New Equipment or New Products (Example)

this problem. Operators should maintain and inspect their machines as well as operate them, and maintenance personnel should not just be specialists in either mechanical or electrical systems but should understand both disciplines. The current situation requires that as many people as possible be trained in maintenance and improvement skills. As people master skills and become involved in planning, measurement, judgment, execution, and improvement, they will develop a sense of satisfaction and achievement.

The Value of TPM

In an age in which so much is made by machines, small variations in equipment performance have a great impact on quality, productivity, cost, speed of delivery, and the potential for workerless operation, as well as a tremendous influence on sales activities. Under these conditions, if engineers select processing equipment and measuring instruments only from catalogs, their machinery can only be equal to or even worse than that used by rival companies. As a result, they can only keep pace with or fall behind their competitors.

Equipment technology and development capabilities have become major factors that demonstrate the strength of a company and set it apart from others. Upgrading equipment technology is an indispensable part of a drive toward computer-integrated manufacturing (CIM) that incorporates comprehensive information systems with equipment automation and factory automation. It is an essential preparation for the pursuit of the ultimate in overall factory efficiency.

This means that there is a need for not only equipment developers and designers but for as many people as possible who have an interest in their equipment and expertise in shop-floor equipment technology. This is the heart of productive maintenance, or PM. Although they may appear to have achieved automation, departments weak in PM can never foster truly profitable equipment technology.

When customers carry out quality audits at factories or when they are visited by salespeople displaying new products (the education of sales engineers for products under development is important here), they often evaluate not only product quality levels but production technology and equipment technology capabilities as well. To win their trust, customers must be given specific explanations of the latter.

TPM Activities

Workplace objectives include raising productivity (P), increasing quality (Q), reducing costs (C), strictly observing delivery deadlines (D), ensuring safety and preventing pollution (S), and boosting worker morale (M), as shown in Figure 1-4. These can easily be confused with *control*, but Figure 1-5 shows how the four inputs — people, machines, materials, and management methods — are interwoven with them.

To boost the output (PQCDSM), improve the level of control over the input. In TPM, aim to improve the result (PQCDSM) by increasing the level of control over equipment. Equipment management often takes a back seat because shop-floor supervisors are too busy trying to put things right *after* the event and sometimes have to operate machines themselves. This indicates a low level of control.

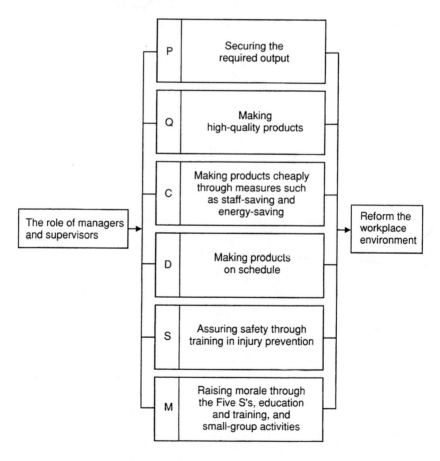

Figure 1-4. The Role of Managers and Supervisors

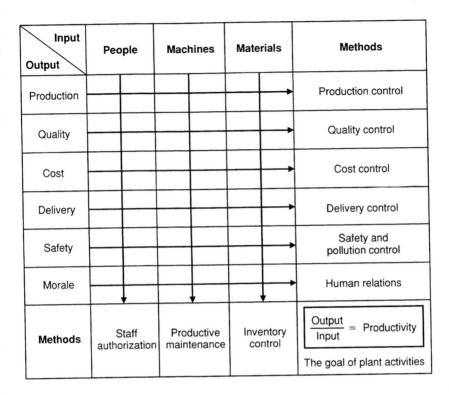

Input Output	People	Machines	Materials	Methods
Production				Production control
Quality				Quality control
Cost				Cost control
Delivery				Delivery control
Safety				Safety and pollution control
Morale				Human relations
Methods	Staff authorization	Productive maintenance	Inventory control	$\dfrac{\text{Output}}{\text{Input}} = \text{Productivity}$ The goal of plant activities

Figure 1-5. The Four Elements of Factory Management

TPM has many facets, but it has six major aims in areas such as discipline, quality, efficiency, and education. It also consists of seven basic activities. Rather than trying to tackle the whole spectrum of activities at once, deal with each in turn. This makes for easier planning and follow-up. These activities are listed in Figure 1-6.

Definition of MQP Management

The subject of this book, quality maintenance, is also known as MQP management. It constitutes one of the pillars of the basic TPM activities previously described. MQP management is sometimes wrongly regarded as mere equipment improvement, but

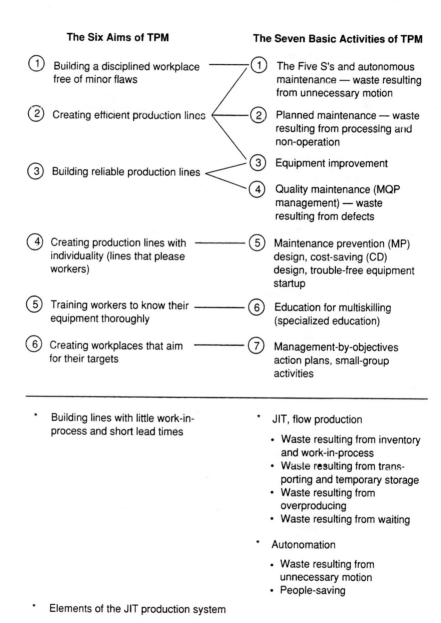

The Six Aims of TPM

① Building a disciplined workplace free of minor flaws

② Creating efficient production lines

③ Building reliable production lines

④ Creating production lines with individuality (lines that please workers)

⑤ Training workers to know their equipment thoroughly

⑥ Creating workplaces that aim for their targets

The Seven Basic Activities of TPM

① The Five S's and autonomous maintenance — waste resulting from unnecessary motion

② Planned maintenance — waste resulting from processing and non-operation

③ Equipment improvement

④ Quality maintenance (MQP management) — waste resulting from defects

⑤ Maintenance prevention (MP) design, cost-saving (CD) design, trouble-free equipment startup

⑥ Education for multiskilling (specialized education)

⑦ Management-by-objectives action plans, small-group activities

---

* Building lines with little work-in-process and short lead times

* Elements of the JIT production system

* JIT, flow production
  • Waste resulting from inventory and work-in-process
  • Waste resulting from transporting and temporary storage
  • Waste resulting from overproducing
  • Waste resulting from waiting

* Autonomation
  • Waste resulting from unnecessary motion
  • People-saving

Figure 1-6. The Aims and Basic Activities of TPM

its philosophy and promotion methodology have been developed systematically, with an eye on the basics.

The aim of MQP management is to achieve perfect quality assurance by identifying and thoroughly controlling the relationship between product quality and the deterioration of both processing conditions and equipment parts. This is done over the complete life cycle of the equipment from development through design, fabrication, purchase, and serviceable life to final scrapping. Equipment is regarded as a means of building in product quality and this includes all kinds of installations including molds, dies, jigs, tools, gauges, automatic quality inspection equipment, testing devices, measuring instruments, and mistake-proofing devices. Perfect quality cannot be guaranteed unless the sources and causes of quality defects are eliminated in advance. To achieve this, find those equipment parts that affect quality, label them "quality components" ("Q components") and manage them carefully. In other words, focus on preemptive control by devising visual controls that facilitate the management of large numbers of equipment parts and make it easier to take action.

Try to identify which processing conditions and quality components cause defects. Also, try to discover the mechanisms by which these defects are created, and how they relate to other factors. Chronic defects are often due to a combination of inferior materials and minor flaws. With such defects, it is important to stress managerial and educational improvements designed to ensure that everyone strictly obeys the rules, rather than place priority on technical improvements. It is vital to build a system that will make this happen.

2

TPM Development at Furukawa Electric

This chapter discusses the introduction of TPM (MQP) at Furukawa Electric and the conditions for its development.

INTRODUCTION TO FURUKAWA ELECTRIC

Furukawa Electric started operations when a copper-smelting plant established in Tokyo in 1884 by Ichibee Furukawa, joined forces with the privately owned Yamada Electric Cable Works. The company adopted its present name in 1920. Furukawa Electric started producing crude copper by electrolysis and has established a solid position in the industry through the integrated production of electric wire and cable with copper and copper-alloy products. It has grown through plant expansion, mergers, and acquisitions, and has steadily diversified into areas such as battery and light metal products by establishing a network of subsidiaries. Furukawa Electric marked its 100th anniversary in 1984. Its spheres of operation are:

- Providing products and systems relating to the transmission, conversion, and processing of energy and information.
- Providing materials for industry and daily life, mainly nonferrous metals and chemicals.
- Business based on the preceding that can contribute to the creation and improvement of a better living environment.

Furukawa Electric is presently capitalized at approximately ¥42,000 million ($300 million), employs 6,900 people, and has an annual turnover of ¥525,700 million ($3.76 billion) with eight factories in Japan and 130 affiliates. It has more than 21 overseas affiliates and is expanding aggressively. It has extended its operations to include a wide range of products such as electric wire and cable, nonferrous metals (aluminum, copper, etc.), plastic products, and materials for electronic components.

COMPANY HISTORY SINCE 1985

Based on an intermediate three-year plan with three fundamental objectives — diversification, greater efficiency, and internationalization — the company forged ahead with a policy of "positive management taking on the challenge of change." For the specific deployment of this policy, each division formulated its own intermediate three-year plan and devised systems to implement it.

Diversification

The basic thread running through Furukawa Electric's diversification policy is how to keep pace with society as it changes under the impact of high technology. With this foundation, the company has promoted further diversification based on distinctive technology that sets it apart from other companies.

It has continued to improve technical capabilities while giving top priority to quality. The research and development topics being tackled for diversification are extremely wide-ranging. They fall into the following major categories:

Optical information systems. Various information systems based on optical fiber and cable technology.

Electronics. Compound semiconductors, materials for bonding wire and lead frames, noble-metal composite contact materials, aluminum magnetic disk substrates, and so on.

New materials. Various superconducting wire materials, shape-memorizing alloys, and new ceramics.

Energy. New types of battery, monitoring and measuring systems, optical composite overhead power transmission lines, and so on.

Increased Efficiency

To ensure that the objectives of the intermediate-range plan were achieved, Furukawa launched a companywide structural reform campaign under the title "NF-87." The following two items were adopted as the campaign's priority themes in 1986:

Effective implementation of NF-87. Continued evolution of the campaign with self-examination to compare current performance with what was commonly accepted at the old Furukawa. Improving production in terms of strategy, objectives, implementation method, and speed. The results of the campaign are to be expressed in terms of actual accounting figures.

Improvement of technical capabilities while giving top priority to quality. Improvement of quality and yield (reduction of material losses) by placing importance on increasing basic theoretical understanding of specific technologies, as well as enhancing quality consciousness and ensuring that fundamental quality-control actions are performed.

Against this background, TPM (MQP) was positioned with quality control (QC) as the activities forming the foundation of the NF-87 campaign.

THE DEVELOPMENT OF TPM

Furukawa Electric introduced TPM in 1977 after learning of its benefits from plant tours and talks by the top management of Yokohama Rubber, a company that was using it with excellent results.

At the time, Furukawa Electric was beset by a host of shop-floor problems as shown in Figure 2-1, and nothing short of a major revolution could extricate it from its predicament. Equipment design placed priority on equipment functions, and much of the new equipment was prone to failure and difficult to use. The design, maintenance, and production divisions were at a stand-off, each insisting on its own viewpoint.

Furukawa Electric also faced a turbulent business climate as the Japanese economy endured the first oil crisis and was forced to shift from the high-growth era to one of low, stable growth. In 1976, a one-year study group — mainly for production section managers and engineering managers responsible for maintenance — was assembled, providing plant managers the chance to give their views. Despite the sense of crisis and the knowledge that something had to be done, some people, as expected, expressed opinions such as: "It isn't just an equipment problem; we also have trouble with quality, personnel, and materials"; "If there are problems with the equipment, the equipment divisions should be able to solve them by themselves"; and "It's obvious what we have to do, so there's no need for a campaign involving the whole company." Nevertheless, there was a strong sense of urgency about how to cope with future equipment and factory automation, and many people realized the need for introducing TPM.

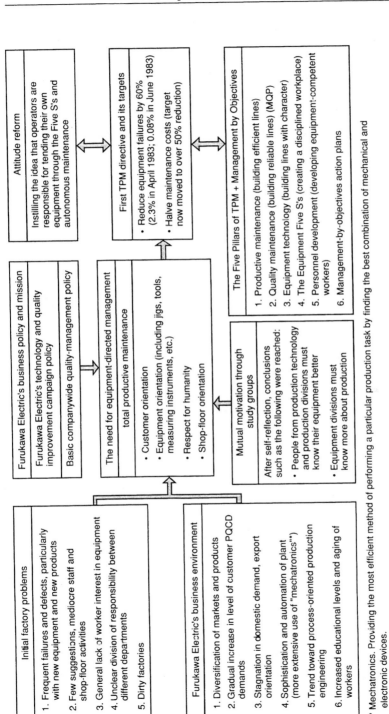

The following tables represent the content of Figure 2-1.

Initial factory problems

1. Frequent failures and defects, particularly with new equipment and new products
2. Few suggestions, mediocre staff and shop-floor activities
3. General lack of worker interest in equipment
4. Unclear division of responsibility between different departments
5. Dirty factories

Furukawa Electric's business environment

1. Diversification of markets and products
2. Gradual increase in level of customer PQCD demands
3. Stagnation in domestic demand, export orientation
4. Sophistication and automation of plant (more extensive use of "mechatronics"*)
5. Trend toward process-oriented production engineering
6. Increased educational levels and aging of workers

Furukawa Electric's business policy and mission

Furukawa Electric's technology and quality improvement campaign policy

Basic companywide quality-management policy

The need for equipment-directed management

total productive maintenance

• Customer orientation
• Equipment orientation (including jigs, tools, measuring instruments, etc.)
• Respect for humanity
• Shop-floor orientation

Mutual motivation through study groups

After self-reflection, conclusions such as the following were reached:

• People from production technology and production divisions must know their equipment better
• Equipment divisions must know more about production

Attitude reform

Instilling the idea that operators are responsible for tending their own equipment through the Five S's and autonomous maintenance

First TPM directive and its targets

• Reduce equipment failures by 60% (2.3% in April 1983; 0.08% in June 1983)
• Halve maintenance costs (target now moved to over 50% reduction)

The Five Pillars of TPM + Management by Objectives

1. Productive maintenance (building efficient lines)
2. Quality maintenance (building reliable lines) (MQP)
3. Equipment technology (building lines with character)
4. The Equipment Five S's (creating a disciplined workplace)
5. Personnel development (developing equipment-competent workers)
6. Management-by-objectives action plans

* Mechatronics. Providing the most efficient method of performing a particular production task by finding the best combination of mechanical and electronic devices.

Figure 2-1. Background to the Progress of TPM Activities (Started in 1977)

The fact that production-technology staff and production-line workers had little interest in their equipment, and the equipment divisions were apathetic about production and product quality were major points for self-reflection.

On orders from top management, it was decided to introduce TPM based on a four-part philosophy of customer orientation, equipment orientation, shop-floor orientation, and respect for humanity. The first target — greatly reducing equipment breakdowns and maintenance costs — was easily achieved. Confidence grew as workers saw that success was attainable with effort. Coupled with the revolutionary notion of looking after one's own equipment through the Five S's* and autonomous maintenance, this was a tremendous gain.

Divisions that had achieved outstanding results by the two-year mark received a president's commendation. This award continued annually thereafter and was extremely effective in keeping the activities vital. The second objective — reducing defects by introducing MQP management — was later extended to include raising output operating rates and yields (reducing material losses) and achieving workerless operation (see Figure 2-2).

Benefits of TPM Deployment

Deployment of TPM produced the following benefits:

- A revolution in attitudes and an increase in maintenance and improvement skills
- Upgrading of equipment technology and specific technology

---

* The Five S's refer to the five Japanese words *seiri* (sorting out), *seiton* (arranging efficiently), *seisō* (checking through cleaning), *seiketsu* (purity), and *shitsuke* (discipline). The Five S's are discussed in Chapter 3.

Indicates action continued ↑

	1976	1977	1978	1979	1980	1981	1982	1983
Directives		First directive — reduce failures and maintenance costs		Second directive — reduce failures, introduce MQP	Third directive — changeover, LCC design	Fourth directive — improve output operating rates		Fifth directive — increase yields, achieve workerless operation
Events	Study groups	Companywide promotion conference	Guidance from specialist	First in-house audit for President's Commendation	Third corporate convention at head office	First factory briefing session		
	Energy-saving campaign				Improvement suggestion scheme			

The Five Pillars of TPM

1. Building efficient lines (productive maintenance)
- MTBF analysis charts
- Autonomous maintenance
- Improved output operating rates
  - zero failures
  - zero idling and minor stoppages
  - zero defects
  - adjustment-free startup
  - single-minute setup
  - zero time on hand
  - zero speed deterioration

(Ultimate equipment utilization)

2. Building reliable lines (quality maintenance)
- MQP management MTBQF analysis charts
- Quality component deployment
- Mistake-proof maps, equipment rearrangement
- Perfect-line certification

(Building in quality through equipment)

3. Building lines with character (equipment technology)
- Workerless operation
- Energy saving
- Smooth startup of new equipment
- In-house fabrication
- LC costing
- Technology mapping

(Building equipment that pleases its operators)

4. Creating a disciplined workplace (the Five S's)
- Contests and competitions
- Mapping of inaccessible places
- "All-Out Five S's"
- Thematic Five S's
- Certification system
- Visual control

(Creating a reliable workplace)

5. Development of equipment-competent workers (transmission and verification of technology, personnel development)
- One-point lessons • Management-by-objectives action plans
- Know-how sheets • Education in maintenance techniques and skills ("Look after your own equipment")

Benefits
- Confidence derived from attainment of high goals
- Mutual trust between different parts of the organization
- Praise from customers for reliable factories, leading to orders
- Switch from dependence on others to self-reliance
- Favorable effects on morale, staff activities, and other activities

Indicators showing beneficial effects
- Failure stoppage severity rate
- Output operating rate
- Good product rate, loss rate
- Energy saving
- Improvement suggestions
- Maintenance costs, etc.

Figure 2-2. Progress, Contents, and Results of TPM Activities

- Efficient system-building
- Disciplined rotation of the PDCA control cycle*

In this way, the introduction and development of TPM led to activities and results that were extremely beneficial.

Remaining Problems

Even with the implementation of TPM, problems remain. Among them:

- Although TPM meets the needs of the factories, coordination with other activities is needed to increase the company's overall profit.
- Efforts easily tend to become focused on the shop floor to the exclusion of other areas.
- If not carefully monitored, maintenance efforts are sometimes neglected, overshadowed by more glamorous improvement projects.
- The vitality of activities tends to drop off, and booster systems are needed. Examples include a certification system, president's targets and commendations for achievement, presentation meetings, president's briefing sessions, going for external awards, and introducing the JIT production system.
- There is a danger of overproducing because of large lot sizes.

INTRODUCING THE JIT PRODUCTION SYSTEM

To further increase profits through QC and TPM improvement activities, the just-in-time production system (JIT) was intro-

---

* The acronym PDCA stands for the four principle steps of total quality control (TQC) management: plan, do, check, and action. For a more detailed description, refer to *Handbook of Quality Tools*, by Ozeki and Asaka, Productivity Press, Cambridge, MA, 1990.

duced. Although JIT is fairly easy to introduce in assembly plants, many problems had to be overcome in processing facilities because of the size of the equipment. JIT aims to make the required items cheaply in exactly the required quantities at the right time. In addition, it aims to shrink stocks, reduce lead times, and bring failures, defects, and other problems to the surface.

The benefits of introducing the JIT production system were:

- Introducing JIT after laying the foundations of QC and TPM magnified the need for improvement. Great benefits resulted from a reduction of lead times, and more efficient use of available workers.
- Processes with inadequate equipment capacity were highlighted, and the need for better output operating rates was increased.
- Failures, defects, and other problems were brought to the surface, and TPM methods became necessary.
- Small-lot production was achieved through production leveling, and a system able to cope with high-variety, low-volume production was created.
- Worker numbers were cut by eliminating wasted motion such as monitoring.

These results show that QC, TPM, and JIT are indispensable for production plants. Using a combination of these three to pursue company objectives leads to true overall plant efficiency management and the development of superb factories (see Figure 2-3).

Which of these three activities — QC, TPM, or JIT — to introduce first depends on a particular company's business results as well as its distinguishing characteristics and historical background. However, the most important guideline is to ensure that all activities meet the factory's needs. Whichever activity is chosen, make a positive effort to use the strengths of the remaining two, provided they do not interfere with the primary activity. Each activity should be implemented over three to five years so that activities are second nature to every individual. The important thing is how much each individual

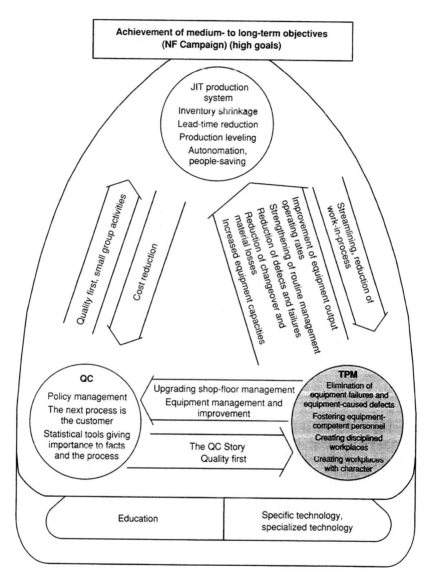

Figure 2-3. Activities for Achieving Targets

changes, how enthusiastic he or she becomes, and how the organization composed of all these individuals grows as an entity. Continuity is the secret of success.

Finally, do not forget that quality and safety come before everything else.

PRECONDITIONS FOR ACHIEVING ZERO QUALITY DEFECTS

This section describes the conditions necessary to attempt zero defects in deploying TPM.

Consider Defect Production a Crime

Defects are of two types: *visible* and *hidden*. Visible defects include those that have always been acknowledged. Extra products must never have to be produced, reworked or manufactured in advance to cope with the generation of these defects.
Hidden defects include the following:

- Reworking or subjecting items to additional processing because they are out of specification after the first run (doubling back).
- Processing to larger-than-standard dimensions because defects occur when the proper dimensions are used (stepping-up).
- Always producing more items than required on the assumption that defects are bound to occur (overproducing).
- Creating superfluous products by producing on spec before a final deadline has been decided (stagnant stock).
- Having to perform destructive testing on too many items because of quality instability.
- Producing defects as a result of confusion during startup (adjustment losses).

Since huge quality costs result from hidden defects that have been largely neglected in the past, taking an interest in them and correcting them can yield significant benefits. Processing factories tend to overlook these losses because scrap resulting from defects can easily be recycled.

Defective products, scrap, and equipment parts that have caused defects must be displayed where everybody can see them. Everyone must be made aware that creating defects is a crime, a source of personal shame, and evidence of lack of responsibility.

Eliminate Defects and Failures

People often complain about insufficient plant capacity during busy periods even though plant capacity is actually reduced by high rates of defect generation and rework. Large numbers of defects can also inconvenience customers and sales staff due to missed delivery dates, rush production staff into dealing with complaints and trying to control delivery schedules, cause loss of faith in the equipment and its operators, lower workplace morale, and increase costs due to wasted time. Creating perfect lines that can guarantee zero quality defects is the basic activity of factory management, and its benefits are enormous.

Identify the Quality Required by Customers

Quality levels required by customers are rising steadily, and anticipating these is the most important task. It has become vital to gather information and increase technical and managerial skills in order to be able to retain the initiative. People must be trained to cope with these higher standards.

Move from Reduction to Elimination

If the view is taken that everything is fine so long as defects decrease, then improvements will not be maintained and defects will start to reappear after two or three years. The job of flushing out every possible cause of defects must be tackled with great tenacity. Defects must be nipped in the bud, and on no account must the same defect be allowed to recur. Only by doing this can defects be eliminated permanently. Rather than taking

satisfaction in a decrease in defects, be satisfied only when defects have disappeared. Adopt this attitude and adamantly resolve to reduce defects to zero.

Perform Inspections and Checks

"I will not accept defects, make defects or pass defects on."
This maxim stresses the use of 100 percent inspection to ensure
that no defects are passed to the next stage of the process. Such
complete screening requires an enormous amount of labor. Because it is impossible to check every item in a final inspection
process, autonomous 100 percent inspection is needed at each
production step. However, all the measuring instruments and
sensors suitable for such inspections have not been developed.
Moreover, major losses can arise if defects occur in long, massive
or bulky products; and defects that cannot be recognized in a
particular operation may only become apparent in subsequent
assembly or final testing. For such reasons, it is difficult to
achieve high reliability with low defect rates on the order of ppm
simply by inspecting *products* after they have been made.

And though equipment reliability increases with full automation, process control, pre-automation and other adjustment
functions, the reliability of control systems and measurement
systems used in this equipment is fundamental, so maintenance
of such systems is essential. Clearly, product inspection alone is
not enough. Ideal processing conditions must be identified as
well as the optimal state of any components that can cause defects. These must be maintained reliably by building in quality
through the process and building in quality through the equipment (see Figure 2-4).

Give Importance to Self-reflection

Particular importance is given to the QC story, which starts
with an examination of the existing situation to identify details

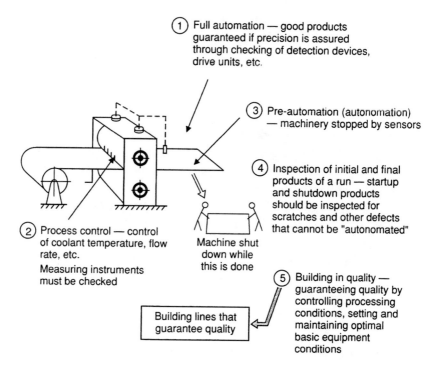

Figure 2-4. **Approaches to Guaranteed Quality and Workerless Operation**

that have not yet developed into problems but are not quite right. This process continues with self-reflection — a great help to examine not only what you are doing wrong but what you are doing right. Look at the reasons why they are right, put observations and impressions in order, and pinpoint areas for deeper study.

To further invigorate the improvement efforts and to spread these activities to all departments, it is important to respect people's feelings and impressions.

Organize for Promotion of Quality

People tend to think that actions taken against defects are the responsibility of a small group of staff. However, goals can never be achieved without the full participation of all employees.

Leadership by division and department managers is indispensable for rapid promotion of the zero defect goal and the achievement of results through deployment of MQP management. All employees, from division and department managers on down, must participate. To realize this goal, create management policies that balance the needs of different divisions, formulate clear plans and objectives, and create a promotion organization designed to communicate these policies to everybody and galvanize them into action. In doing so, consider the following:

- Concern and leadership from top management — top management audits, presentation meetings, briefing sessions, etc.
- Development of and support by full-time facilitators
- Guidance by outside consultants
- Lateral dissemination within divisions by division managers — encouragement, stimulation of competition, etc.

Work-team leaders play the main role in daily management of policies and objectives passed on to the workplace.

It is important to note that, while stressing the severe conditions in which Furukawa Electric found itself and the need to boost its profits, it was emphasized that, unless members of the group pulled their own weight, they would create problems for their colleagues and ultimately themselves. Therefore, leaders set targets that would not be reached unless everyone tried their hardest. Moreover, the leaders tried to ensure that full participation would yield excellent results and a distinct sense of achievement and satisfaction.

3

Deploying the Five S's and Autonomous Quality Maintenance

This chapter discusses in concrete terms the promotion of the Five S's and autonomous quality maintenance, the foundations of MQP management. As with other management activities, MQP management depends on creating a disciplined workplace.

THE FIVE S'S

Even production managers at factories with a relatively high level of control believe the most worrisome problem on the shop floor to be whether people will observe what has been decided and do things as agreed. Creating a disciplined workplace in which people follow the rules and perform tasks in the agreed way is the permanent, basic problem of shop-floor activities. Once this basic foundation has been laid, improvement work can proceed efficiently; if it is not, the results tend to be minimal.

Creating this disciplined workplace requires that people recognize their responsibilities and change their behavior; and

31

the most effective way to change behavior is through education and training. In the early stages of training in the Five S's, excuses and grumbling are common. A frequent grumbling: "Will these Five S's make any money?"

The Five S's refer to the five Japanese words *seiri* (sorting out), *seiton* (arranging efficiently), *seisō* (checking through cleaning), *seiketsu* (purity), and *shitsuke* (discipline). Anyone can practice them, and although these activities seem easy, they are actually difficult to put into practice. If everyone practices them, however, the result is a disciplined workplace (see Figure 3-1). Promoting the Five S's must be done with the conviction that they will save money and that ways can be found to make them profitable on other fronts. The Five S's have proved to be the best activities for reforming everybody's outlook.

When putting the Five S's into effect, decide each worker's allotted tasks, give each a sense of responsibility, and list aims and established standards as shown in Figure 3-2. The Five S's are a shop-floor activity that is a form of training. A little ingenuity in how that training is carried out will yield all sorts of good results.

Anybody can adopt the Five S's, and whoever does can derive a great deal of satisfaction from them. As training progresses, earlier grumblings give way to optimism and pride.

The basis of MQP management as a means of eliminating defects is to build a system in which people steadfastly follow stringent standards. This can be done by using the Five S's as a form of managerial and educational improvement. Such a system produces lasting benefits by exposing numerous minor flaws that contribute to defects and failures.

Goals of the Five S's

When the Five S's are first introduced, it is surprisingly difficult to ensure that everyone does them thoroughly. People can easily head off in the wrong direction.

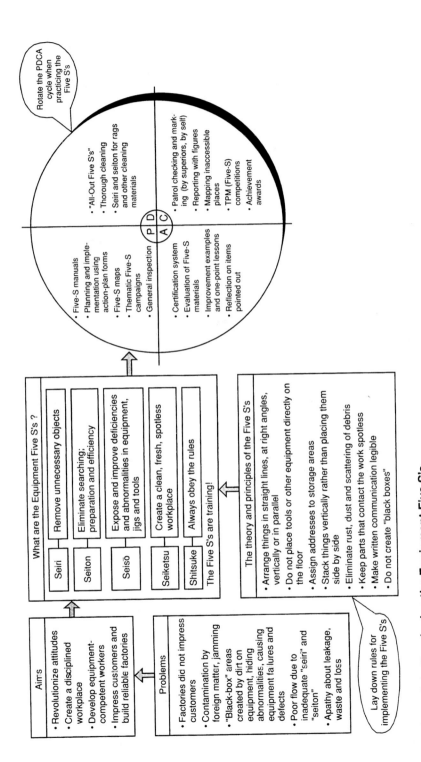

Figure 3-1. Developing the Equipment Five S's

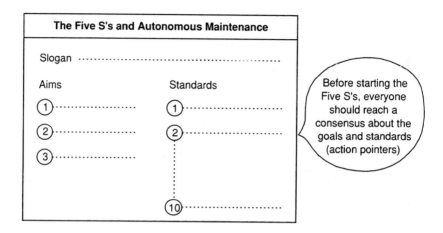

Figure 3-2. The Five S's and Autonomous Maintenance

In developing the Five S's, it is important that all study their objectives, state them, and ensure that they understand them. If the Five S's are started with a happy-go-lucky approach, they will soon come to a dead end. In addressing the Five S's, it helps to create a promotion plan and organization that will have a dynamic impact and convince people that this is an activity in which they must all be involved. Also useful are discussions on the best ways of ensuring that the activities catch on.

Some of the goals of the Five S's are:

Create a disciplined workplace. Creating a disciplined workplace in which everyone scrupulously observes the rules is an essential fundamental of shop-floor management, and practicing the Five S's is the most effective way of achieving it. The idea is that, if people cannot cooperate to do a simple task like housekeeping, they are unlikely to be able to follow standard work procedures or other regulations (see Figure 3-3). One way to ensure that everyone understands this is to start by having them decide for themselves their particular roles in the third of the Five S's, *seisō* (checking through cleaning). Unless people accept their allotted tasks, the work to be done will always be directed from above.

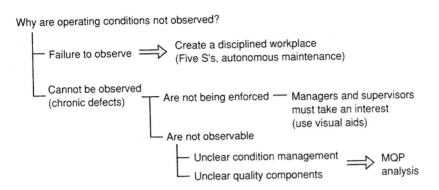

Figure 3-3. Observing Operating Conditions

Use cleaning to check for poor functioning and minor flaws. Seisō is not just cleaning. It means using cleaning to discover and expose the malfunctions, abnormalities, and minor flaws that presage failures and defects. It also means finding the sources of these problems and exposing locations that are usually difficult to inspect. During cleaning and inspection, workers often discover small abnormalities liable to develop into major problems. These discoveries warrant attention from superiors.

Establish visual controls. Inspection is simplified by making hard-to-clean and hard-to-inspect places more accessible and providing visual controls such as gauge marks and match marks that will enable anyone to understand the shop-floor situation at a glance. This helps create a workplace that tells its own story, and it improves inspection efficiency. In addition, it enables everyone — from division and department managers on down — to get involved in checking and improvement. Building in quality starts with visual observation and measurement.

Develop equipment-competent workers. The Five S's and autonomous maintenance are used to get as many people as possible interested in caring for their equipment. The knowledge and skills they obtain through this training helps improve their judgment and continuous improvement abilities.

Take preemptive action. Another goal is to change people's attitudes and make them realize the importance of precautionary, preventive action. This is done by starting shop-floor Five-S activities as a first step toward tackling problems that require everybody's cooperation.

Improve standardization and external setup. Seiri (sorting out) consists of separating what is needed from what is not needed, placing regularly used items close at hand, occasionally used items in an intermediate store and rarely used items at a distance. *Seiton* (arranging efficiently) consists of arranging items so that those needed can be accessed quickly at the right time, in the right quantity, and in good condition. The procedure consists of standardizing and laying out the necessary tools, jigs, dies, materials, fixtures, etc. in advance of the setup operation in the required position and in the specified condition. This is why *seiri* and *seiton* are synonymous with efficiency and are the preconditions for quick changeover.

Promote sales. The role of the factory in sales promotion is becoming more important every year, and the Five S's are an effective means of raising the level of control on the factory floor and increasing worker morale. This enables you to show potential customers around and convince them they can trust the quality of the products and buy with confidence. This is the best possible type of sales promotion; it is based on the notion that the factory floor itself is a saleable product.

Promoting and Implementing the Five S's

In promoting the Five S's, it is important that everyone discuss them carefully to clarify their goals and objectives, understand the theory and principles behind them, and appreciate the ideal conditions they make possible. The brand of Five S's that is instilled must suit the characteristics of a particular factory or workplace, and should be launched without asking questions such as, "Will they be profitable?" If practiced with conviction and persistence, their benefits will soon become apparent.

Initial Cleaning (Seisō)

Equipment is checked by actually touching and cleaning it. After thorough preparation, division and department managers take the lead by carrying out an initial cleaning of a model line. Deficiencies are located and corrected. They include such problems as rust, dirt, dust, spraying of water, scattering of oil or powder, leakage of compressed air or steam, uneven temperature distribution, illegible signs, loose nuts and bolts, improper lubrication, unnecessary objects left lying around, and misplaced objects. If the line is observed carefully beforehand and the necessary materials are prepared before cleaning starts, a minimum of several dozen minor flaws and abnormalities can be corrected during each round of cleaning. Data on these should be analyzed and kept for future reference.

Five-S Manuals and Calendars

Maintain and improve the condition of the line after initial cleaning by daily practice of the Five S's using Five-S manuals and calendars that focus on a different area each day.

Allocating Responsibility

For each item of equipment, decide how the work is to be shared. Make it obvious who is responsible by attaching a card to the equipment with a slogan such as "I'm responsible for this machine" and the person's name. Everybody can find some excuse for not doing something so oblige people to carry out the Five S's by clearly allocating responsibility (see Figure 3-4).

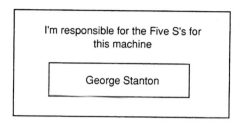

Figure 3-4. My Share of the Work

"All-Out Five S's"

For even deeper inculcation of discipline in the workplace, introduce the practice of "All-Out Five S's" ("My Five-Minute Five S's"). For this, each worker chooses a Five-S item for himself or herself in addition to the items on the Five-S calendar and works out what preparations are needed and what can actually be done and checked in five minutes.

Key Points in Promoting Seisō *(checking through cleaning)*

- Cleaning is checking. Try touching the equipment. Try polishing it. Instead of painting it, shine it and run your hands over it. Detect small flaws and abnormalities this way.
- Ask workers to describe five of their Five-S and autonomous maintenance tasks. If they can answer satisfactorily, the workplace has reached a fairly high level.
- The equipment you are using will not last long, and you cannot continue building in quality with it if it is smeared with grease and dust and you do not know when you last cleaned it. Be prepared to look after your own equipment.
- *Seisō* will not succeed through the efforts of a small number of staff. It only works if all employees obey the Five-S rules, and it relies on each individual's autono-mous maintenance efforts. The type of cleaning that results from employing more cleaners is meaningless.

- Extremely dirty factories need one or two full-scale cleanings, with everybody coming in voluntarily on their day off. Preparation is very important when this is done.
- Counting the number of minor flaws, finding sources of contamination, and locating hard-to-check places is important. The goal is not merely to get things clean; it is also important to clarify any points of uncertainty and eliminate "black boxes" by grilling your bosses, repeatedly asking "Why?"
- Make extensive use of photographs, overhead transparencies, videos, and before-and-after comparisons.
- Everybody, including the plant manager and staff, should take part in cleaning. Division and department managers must take responsibility for the condition of their factory.
- Take your time. Introduce new rules one at a time. If too many items are introduced at once, there is a danger that they will only be carried out halfheartedly.
- When a minor flaw or deficiency is detected, make sure that everyone knows about it by affixing a TPM picture card to the spot where it was found. Then, as much as possible, try to correct it yourself (see Figures 3-5 and 3-6). Discover the sources of oil leakage, chips, and other abnormalities and deal with them promptly.
- Use ingenuity to ensure that the Five S's are profitable.
- Start by taking action. Once it is done, you will undoubtedly be glad.
- Rotate the PDCA cycle with the Five S's as well (at the organizational and individual levels).
- Make sure that the philosophy and objectives of the Five S's are clear.
- Start by building a model line.
- Make everything visible.
- Be scrupulous about visual controls. Half measures are useless. Any painting or writing must be done properly.

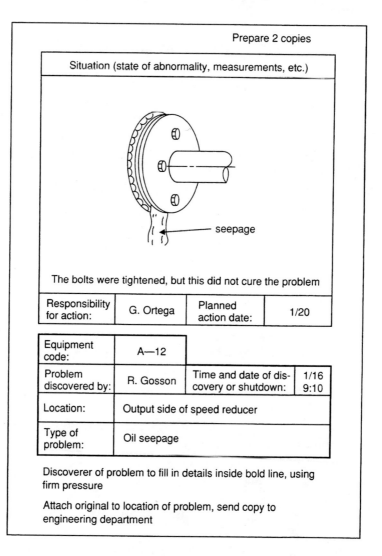

Prepare 2 copies

Situation (state of abnormality, measurements, etc.)			

seepage

The bolts were tightened, but this did not cure the problem

Responsibility for action:	G. Ortega	Planned action date:	1/20

Equipment code:	A—12		
Problem discovered by:	R. Gosson	Time and date of discovery or shutdown:	1/16 9:10
Location:	Output side of speed reducer		
Type of problem:	Oil seepage		

Discoverer of problem to fill in details inside bold line, using firm pressure

Attach original to location of problem, send copy to engineering department

Figure 3-5. TPM Picture Card for Exposing Minor Flaws

Total number of leaks detected: 147

Proportion of leaks by type

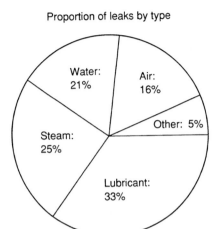

Figure 3-6. Leak Analysis

- When collecting data, do it with action in mind. Give importance to effort-oriented, action-oriented objectives and data.
- Make sure that data serves a purpose and does not become a useless collection of numbers.
- Treat decisions with respect. Make rules. If equipment is very dirty, hold an *action day* to deal with it.
- Make time for the Five S's.
- Give importance to Five-S techniques, such as actions against the source of contamination.
- Be enthusiastic. Practice the Five S's on your assigned equipment to the best of your ability.
- Give importance to communication. Share your experience with others by such methods as one-point lessons.
- The Five S's are the acid test of whether rules can be followed.

- Do not just point out whether the equipment is clean or not. The important thing is how the Five S's change people's behavior.
- Discover the most effective cleaning materials and treat them with care. Make your own cleaning tools and storage racks.
- Provide as many containers of rags (equipment handkerchiefs) as possible, so that anyone can use them at any time. A *quick wipe* is important.

Ideas for Visual Control

Checklists are often used for equipment inspection, and many division and department managers feel reassured when they look at these and see the check marks, believing this to mean that the Five S's are being carried out. However, the same shop floor often has a low Five-S level with frequent failures and defects. In MQP management, you must make the inspection of large numbers of components as easy as possible. To do this, use visual control, which makes the shop floor speak for itself and allows everyone to see what is happening.

Exercise your ingenuity and conduct research to make the shop floor an easily understandable place, where anyone can see what, where, and how anything is happening, and what, when, and where action is being taken to deal with abnormalities.

Examples of Visual Control

- Identifying electrical wiring (100V, 200V)
- Labeling switches
- Clear marking of trash cans and containers for defective products
- Warning notices
- Labeling of storage racks with location and description of contents
- Color-coding hoisting wires by rated load

- Identifying equipment under repair or idle
- Standardizing notices (height, position, size, color, etc.)
- Standardizing locations for objects, designating storage areas
- Identifying piping, indicating flow direction in pipes, labeling open and closed positions of valves

Five-S Patrols

Support from division and department managers and staff is important for efficient promotion of the Five S's. Promotional activities can include:

- Competitions for the best maintenance carts, changeover carts, cleaning tools, and other Five-S equipment
- One-point lesson-sheet competitions
- Competitions for accessing spare parts and other supplies within 30 seconds
- Regular Five-S patrols
- Marking and ranking using Five-S checklists

Five-S patrols consist of managers conducting audits by touring each workplace once or twice a month and pointing out several dozen improvement items per person. In the initial stages, there will be many items such as those shown in Figure 3-7, i.e., incorrect location of objects, dirt, inadequate labeling, improper lubrication, and damage.

Identifying and Following Up Five-S Results

The results achieved by promoting the Five S's should be identified numerically in terms of the following items, which should then be summarized and used in the next step:

- Number of minor flaws detected (= number of TPM picture cards)
- Amount of unnecessary materials and dead stock scrapped

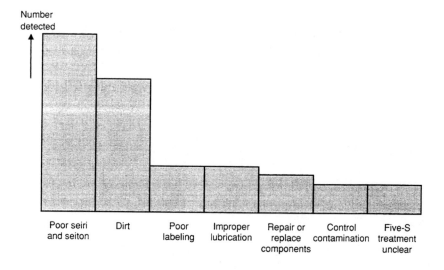

Figure 3-7. Deficiencies Detected During Patrols

- Reduction in the amount of lubricant used
- Number of one-point lesson sheets prepared and used
- Number of improvement examples and case-study sheets prepared
- Number of agreed-upon standards
- Number of inspection points and deficiencies detected
- Number of know-how sheets prepared
- Number of improvement suggestions submitted
- Number of circle and team meetings held
- Number and rate of autonomous maintenance jobs performed
- Five-S scores (average)

FROM THE FIVE S'S TO AUTONOMOUS QUALITY MAINTENANCE

The Five S's, with everybody's participation, are designed to create a disciplined workplace. Once the foundation of these activities has been laid, the next step is to evolve quality-oriented autonomous maintenance. Molds, dies, jigs, gauges, automatic quality inspection equipment, testing devices, industrial measuring instruments, mistake-proofing devices, cutting tools, and other devices are all means of building in product quality — and minor flaws and abnormalities in these ultimately result in failures and defects (see Figure 3-8). Quality-oriented autonomous maintenance is a way of detecting and correcting such problems through daily cleaning and inspection initiated by the workers.

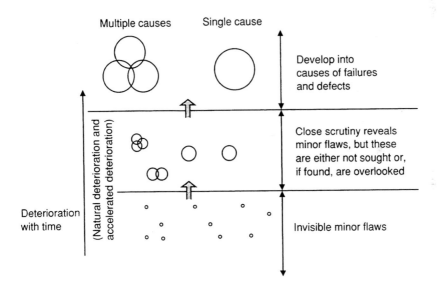

Figure 3-8. Detection and Improvement of Minor Flaws

The aim is not merely to track and repair minor flaws and abnormalities, but also to understand the function of each component and how it works. Positive steps must be taken to determine not only the best method of inspecting a component, but also why it must be inspected and what repercussions there would be if it failed, whether it can be prevented from failing, and anything else worth noting about it. Everybody must realize that study is necessary if they are to go beyond merely practicing the Five S's to the next phase of action.

The various systems developed for implementing the Five S's are used without modification for autonomous maintenance.

The Role of the Operator in Autonomous Maintenance

Use the Five S's and autonomous maintenance to ensure that maintenance philosophy and techniques are disseminated to all members of the production divisions. Start by tackling basic routine autonomous maintenance activities for preventing deterioration — activities such as cleaning, lubricating, and bolt tightening. Operators are expected to perform a wide variety of tasks including:

- Correct operation, changeover, and servicing, as well as multiprocess handling
- Daily cleaning and inspection and participation in planned maintenance
- Prompt detection of abnormalities and accurate, swift reporting, and taking corrective action
- Minor maintenance jobs and improvements on equipment
- Inspection and data-recording on output and quality
- Keeping work flowing on schedule
- Pursuing cost-reduction targets and other goals
- Participating in education, small-group activities and suggestion schemes

To become truly competent, each individual operator must fully understand and accept the importance of autonomous maintenance and develop a liking for and interest in his or her equipment through education, training, and practice.

Eight Steps to Autonomous Quality Maintenance

Autonomous maintenance activities with everybody participating and operators taking the main role are very complex, and must evolve and become established over a long period. Because of this, they are promoted according to the steps shown in Figure 3-9.

Step 1: Initial Cleaning

The system for deploying the Five S's is used without modification for autonomous quality maintenance. Initial cleaning is carried out on equipment, and problems such as wear and tear, excessive play, looseness, deformation, surface damage, and rust are exposed and corrected. Autonomous maintenance calendars are then prepared and used for follow-up (see Figure 3-10).

Examples of specific steps taken to promote initial cleaning, together with comments from the participants, appear in Figures 3-11 and 3-12.

Step 2: Tightening and Lubrication

The aim of this step is to prevent the two most common causes of failures and defects: loose nuts and bolts and improper lubrication.

Tightening. The goal is to tighten all important nuts, bolts, and screws that could easily work loose and contribute to failures or compromise safety. When this is done, the total number found loose and tightened is displayed for easy reference during the next round of tightening (see Figure 3-13). Important nuts, bolts, or screws found loose are provided with white matchmarks to make any future slackening easy to spot. During the second round of tightening, items found to have worked

	Autonomous Maintenance	Five S's and visual control	Elimination of failures	Elimination of defects	Autonomous maintenance education
Step 1	• Initial cleaning • Nomination of PM leaders • Exposure and improvement of deficiencies and abnormalities • Preparation of autonomous maintenance calendars • Cleaning of work-route lines	Decide on method of developing Five S's (goals, theory, principles, etc.) Seisō (checking through cleaning), seiri (sorting out) and seiton (arranging efficiently)	Failure data collection and analysis	Defect data collection and analysis	• Training for introduction of autonomous maintenance • Autonomous maintenance manuals • Education by one-point lessons (OPL) • OPL rallies
Step 2	Tightening and lubrication	• Visual control	• Data on failures due to improper lubrication • Lubrication management		• Education on tightening and lubrication
Step 3	Making improvements. Actions to eliminate sources of contamination and scattering, and to increase accessibility of places that are hard to reach		• Participation in planned maintenance	• Collection and analysis of data on scratches, dents, and other surface defects • Participation in planned maintenance	• Five-S techniques and improvement • Training in welding skills
Step 4	Preparation of cleaning and lubrication standards	• Visual control	• Meantime between failure (MTBF) analysis		
Step 5	General inspection		• Frequent failures	• Frequent defects	• Practical training in mechanical elements

Step 6	Seiri (sorting out) and seiton (arranging efficiently). Efficient arrangement of tools and parts.	• Stationing and labeling	• Spare parts control • Servicing of maintenance carts	• Control of measuring instruments and gauges	
Step 7	Autonomous inspection of quality components	• Labeling of quality components		• Meantime between quality failure (MTBQF) analysis analysis • Measurement control	
Step 8	Thorough inculcation of self-management				Collection of improvement case studies
Intermediate and advanced MQP management				MQP management 1. Equipment improvement 2. Planned quality maintenance 3. Measures against idling and minor stoppages 4. Production that is free of adjustments and right the first time 5. Inculcation of accuracy control [Building assured-quality, workerless lines]	Raising improvement abilities by means of improvement teams Building original equipment by in-house fabrication

Figure 3-9. The Autonomous Quality Maintenance Steps in Relation to Other Activities

No.	Maintenance item		No. of sites	①	2	3	4	5	6	⑦
1	FRLs	Check oil level, drain, disassemble and service	7							
2	Lubrication of grease nipples		25							
3	Rust	Paint, apply corrosion inhibitor	—							
4	Leakage (draw maps)	Compressed air, gas, water, oil	—							
5	Scatter (draw maps)	Chips, dust, fumes	—							
6	Sight-glasses	Oil level, oil contamination	12							
7	Pressure	Pressure gauge marks	20							
8	Temperature (difference)	Gauges, thermosensitive labels	18							
9	Flow	Water, oil	6		●					
10	Vibration	Measurement points and recording	8							
11	Tightening	Matchmarks, seals	21							
12	Cleaning work-route	Foreign matter, dirt, deformation, malfunctions	—						●	
13	Photocells, limit switches	Matchmarks, actuation check	30					●		
14	Control panels	Dirt, filters	3				⊗ Loose door			
15	Wiring	Damage, dirt	—							
16	Hydraulic hoses	Cracks	5							
17	Belts, chains	Wear, slackness	12							

Figure 3-10. Autonomous Maintenance Calendar

Equipment name

Day																								Person responsible
⑧	9	10	11	12	13	⑭	⑮	16	17	18	19	20	21	22	23	24	25	26	27	28	29	㉚	㉛	
								●																Robinson
●																								"
																		●						"
																	●							"
												●												"
		⊗																						"
Contaminated in two places																								
									●															"
										●														Jones
															●									"
																				●				"
											●													"
					●								⊗								●			"
Guides defective in two places																								
																								Peters
																								"
			●																					"
				●											⊗									Decker
Cracked in one place																								
																			●					"

Step 1: Identify current status (preparation)
- Occurrence of failures and quality defects
- Current PM implementation status

Step 2: Shop floor observation (preparation)
- Using reference materials, check difference between actual and desired situation
- Expose slight defects and problems

Step 3: Collate data on slight defects (preparation)
- List and clarify countermeasures
- Prepare tools

Step 4: Shop floor cleaning and inspection (improvement)
- Discovery of additional slight defects (action)

Step 5: Organization and preparation of standards
- Collate data on slight defects
- Prepare standard documents, calendars, and maps

Step 6: Education and self-reflection
- Preparation and teaching of one-point lessons
- Clarify discoveries

Figure 3-11. Steps for Implementing Initial Cleaning

loose again are provided with red matchmarks to show that they require special attention.

Although factories often put matchmarks on all nuts and bolts, they may also be put only on those that are of particular importance and require special attention. These are noted in the manuals.

Lubrication. Sliding or rotating surfaces soon seize up if not properly lubricated. Lubrication is the most important aspect of equipment maintenance and control. A breakdown that occurs because of improper lubrication is a serious embarrassment. To ensure that lubrication is performed properly without any omissions, make the following preparations:

- "The initial cleaning we did today was very worthwhile, since we made many specific improvements. It was a good starting point."

- "Up 'til now, we have made many decisions that have then been ignored. From now on, I hope everyone will work together to firmly establish the rules."

- "I intend to work with shop-floor operators toward the thorough implementation of spare parts control."

- "I'm going to make the most of this initial cleaning and not let it go to waste."

- "I became keenly aware of the serious effect that equipment maintenance has on quality, and I'm going to make even more effort in the future."

- "Up till now, this kind of activity has been too much of a formality. This time, we have made it easy to do, so let's do it properly."

- "Quality and the Five S's are synonymous. I felt strongly that our efforts up to now have been sloppy and amateurish."

- "I'm going to check the state of progress on the calendar every week. There'll be no excuses for not achieving the targets!" (department manager).

- "I'm going to be the driving force behind our PM activities and provide support, criticism and encouragement to help the shop-floor, maintenance and production technology divisions do their utmost" (division manager).

Figure 3-12. Comments by Initial Cleaning Participants

Equipment name: AB-1	Tightening record		
Month/ Year	Total number tightened	Number found loose	Looseness rate
June 1983	9,852	981	10.0%
September	7,211	197	2.7
March 1984	5,112	31	0.6

Matchmarks:
White line (width 2 mm)
Use a red line for items
found loose more than
once

Figure 3-13. Tightening Record and Matchmarks

- Clearly identify the lubricants to be used and provide designated storage areas (substations) for them.
- Decide on a color (green, brown, red, etc.) for each lubricant, and color-code containers, dipsticks, and lubrication points (visual control).
- Study different types of lubricant inlets and lubrication techniques. Sometimes pipes become blocked with oil or grease, preventing fresh lubricant from reaching the appropriate components. Guard against over-lubricating.
- Prepare lubrication maps. To ensure that no lubrication points are overlooked, check and map their locations and numbers. It is also a good idea to note lubrication routes and lubrication times on these maps.
- Label and color-code each lubrication inlet to indicate type of lubricant to be used and lubrication interval; then lubricate regularly.

Also, pay attention to the amount and cleanliness of fluids used in gearboxes and hydraulic units. Provide oil gauges with limit marks and keep the glass clean so they are easy to check. Since it is unreasonable to expect an entire machine to be kept spotless, use visual controls to highlight the vital functional parts and take pains to clean and inspect these properly (see Figure 3-14).

Step 3: Making Improvements

The aim of this step is to take action against sources of contamination, against scattering of debris, and to carry out improvements that simplify working on places that are hard to clean, inspect, lubricate, and tighten. By doing so, you prevent equipment that has been cleaned from becoming soiled again. This step is important, but there is a tendency to leave it only half done. This step is, however, the first in inculcating the basic philosophy of PM — maintaining perfection by eliminating the sources of trouble and contamination.

Example of bearing lubrication

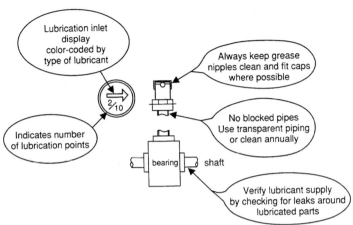

Visual controls for oil gauges

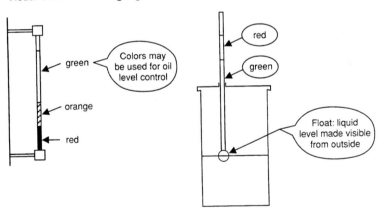

Figure 3-14. Visual Controls for Lubrication

Action against sources of contamination. It is often the case that equipment soon becomes dirty again no matter how frequently it is cleaned. Start by observing the workplace closely to find out which parts get dirty, what makes them dirty, when and why they get dirty and how dirty they get. Draw maps that show the extent and location of contamination by oil, water, dust, chips, ink, mist, fumes, rust, iron filings, and so on. For example, measure the amount of dust that falls by placing pieces of white paper at strategic points and seeing how much dust collects in a fixed period of time. Obtain an overall picture by plotting the results on a map of contamination sources (see Figure 3-15).

Action against scattering of debris. Devise effective measures not only for preventing contamination in the first place, but also for preventing it from being scattered around if it does occur (see Figures 3-16 and 3-17).

- Devise machining methods that do not generate contamination
- Prevent escape of contamination by sealing off the source
- Ensure that seals are working properly
- Check for blocked piping and loose nuts and bolts
- Enclose contamination sources as tightly as possible with localized covers
- Provide receptacles to catch drips
- Use air blowers to force contamination toward designated receptacles
- Prevent spillage by eliminating the need to transport materials
- Use dust collectors with inlets of carefully designed shape and orientation
- Devise efficient washing methods

Start campaigns with appealing titles to encourage everyone to make a concerted effort to carry out these activities. Examples might include:

- "Cover-up Campaign" (Example: antispatter covers for arc welding)
- "Hole-Covering Campaign"
- "Oil-Pan Campaign" and "Oil-Pan Elimination Campaign"

Trouble due to foreign
matter, dust, dirt, etc.

The floor must be cleaned
until no dirt can be
detected on stroking with
the palm of the hand or a
white glove

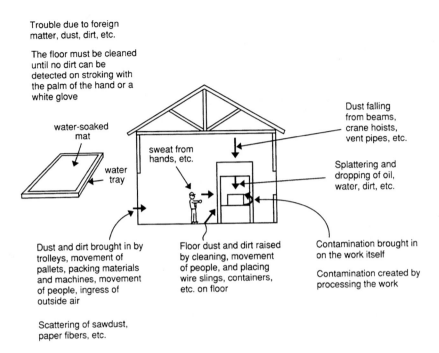

Dust falling
from beams,
crane hoists,
vent pipes, etc.

Splattering and
dropping of oil,
water, dirt, etc.

Dust and dirt brought in by
trolleys, movement of
pallets, packing materials
and machines, movement
of people, ingress of
outside air

Floor dust and dirt raised
by cleaning, movement
of people, and placing
wire slings, containers,
etc. on floor

Contamination brought in
on the work itself

Contamination created by
processing the work

Scattering of sawdust,
paper fibers, etc.

Countermeasures

1. Wax or paint floors
2. Keep ceiling beams and cranes clean
3. Provide wet mats at entrances
4. Fit wheels with brushes or rags
5. Ensure that interior of workshop is not at negative pressure
6. Do not install large-capacity ventilation equipment unless
   absolutely necessary

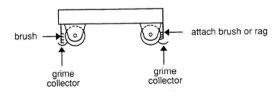

**Figure 3-15. Measures Against Sources of Contamination in Precision
Machine Shops**

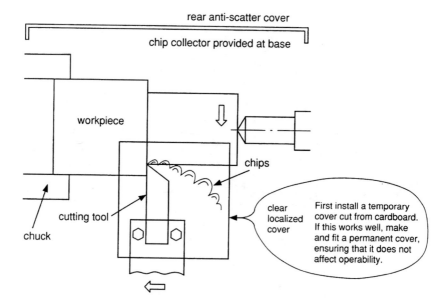

Figure 3-16. Localized Cover for Cutting Process

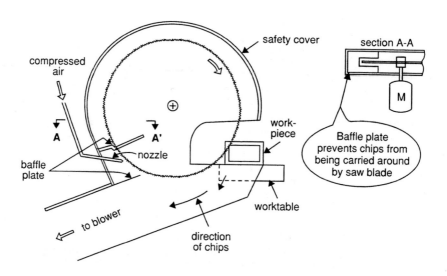

Figure 3-17. Anti-Scatter Measures for Sawing-Machine Chips

Action to increase accessibility of places that are hard to reach. This makes it easy to clean and inspect key parts by simply walking around the equipment during daily inspections and patrols while the machine is running.

- Remove doors as much as possible, or make them easy to remove
- Install inspection ports in doors and replace steel doors with clear plastic ones
- Shift the position of components that must be inspected so they can be seen from outside

Cleaning the work-route line and eliminating sources of contamination. Scratches, deformation, and other damage can be prevented by cleaning the route along which the work passes as well as the surrounding area. Refer to Figure 3-18 and Figure 3-19. To prevent future contamination, track and eliminate the sources of foreign matter.

Step 4: Prepare Standards for Cleaning and Inspection

Based on the experience gained in Step 3, prepare inspection standards with the aim of maintaining and establishing the optimal basic conditions for quality (see Figure 3-20).

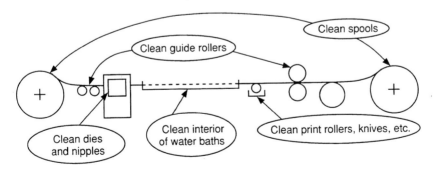

- Keep area within 20 cm of product spotless
- Try to reduce contamination caused by falling dust

Figure 3-18. Contact-Goods Five S's for Extrusion Line

Topic: Detect deficiencies before cleaning	
Explanation: What are "Work-Route Five S's"	**Photograph or diagram of deficiency**
foreign matter sticking to work 	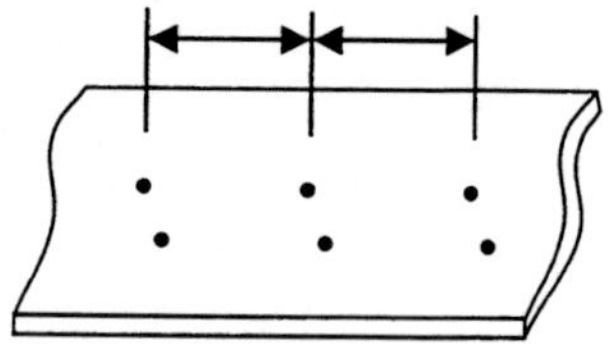 regular occurrence at constant spacing
Causes Place emphasis on the contamination itself (adherence of foreign matter) and action required against its source (recurrence prevention or precautionary measure) rather than on cleaning (action dealing only with the result). Defects cannot be eliminated if action deals only with the result (cleaning is inspection).	**Schematic diagram**
Countermeasures 1. With bare hands, confirm presence of foreign matter 2. Study shapes and makeup of foreign matter 3. Discover root causes 4. Check for dirt in area	

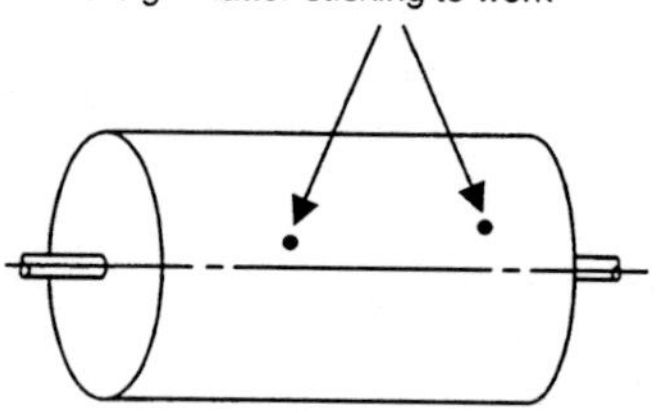

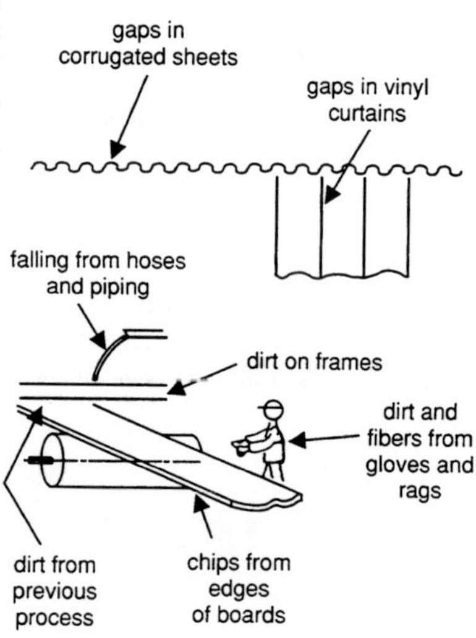

Figure 3-19. **Work-Route Five S's (One-Point Lesson)**

Strict adherence to many standards, including those for cleaning, inspection, and lubrication, is easier to discuss than to apply. No matter how good the standards may be, it is a big mistake to think that they will be observed if they are prepared by the staff and presented to the shop-floor workers without modification. Much better results will be obtained if those who must obey the standards use initial cleaning to decide for themselves what rules to follow.

In preparing standards, pay close attention to procedures such as using diagrams as maps, inspecting by touching with bare hands, setting standard values, clarifying the relation between equipment and quality, clearly stating the numbers and intervals of inspections, and using visual controls (see Figure 3-21).

Step 5: General Inspection

Although inspection was established to some extent in the previous step, this step takes it further. Components that fail frequently are identified from the defect data and investigated more closely. A general inspection is performed to identify problem areas that were missed in previous inspections. This helps to reveal inadequacies in inspection methods themselves.

Since many aspects of equipment deterioration are hard to quantify or make measurable, an inspection depends greatly on the five senses. Familiarity with the equipment is therefore crucial. For selected machine elements, prepare aids such as autonomous maintenance manuals and cutaway models, then train operators in the functions, mechanisms, and methods required to inspect them.

When carrying out general inspection, try to discover slight defects and abnormalities. When there are many components to inspect, it helps to make maps showing their numbers and locations. To ensure that improvements are maintained, regularly review the standards, evaluate inspection skills, and provide retraining in deficient areas.

Division   Equipment

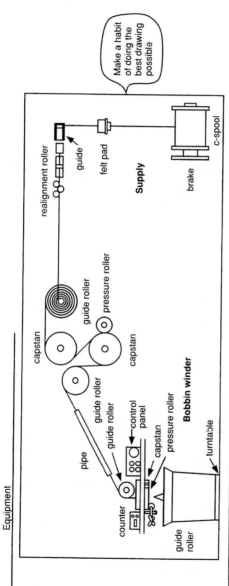

No.	Item	Phenomenon	Method	Standard	Effect on quality	Number	Type of control	Interval	Department responsible	Recurrence prevention
1	C-spools	Dirt and surface damage	Touch	Check for anything that feels unusual	Scratches	All	—	When returning	Production	
2	Felt pads	Copper or iron powder	Look	Limit sample	"	5	—	Once a day	"	
3	Guide and realignment rollers	Faulty rotation	Look	Check that mark is rotating	Scratches, faulty winding	14 × 5	—	Once a day	"	

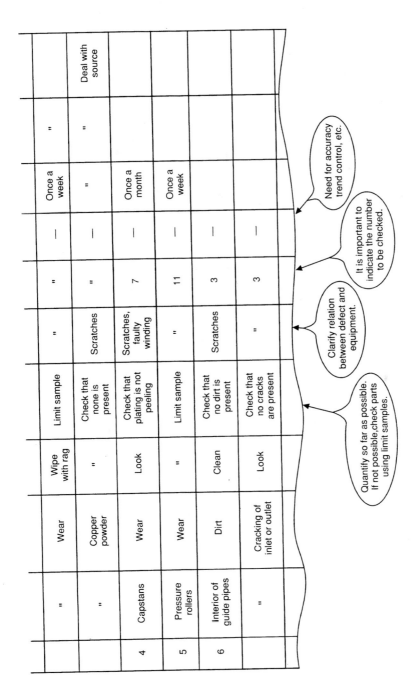

Figure 3-20. Cleaning and Inspection Standard

Piping

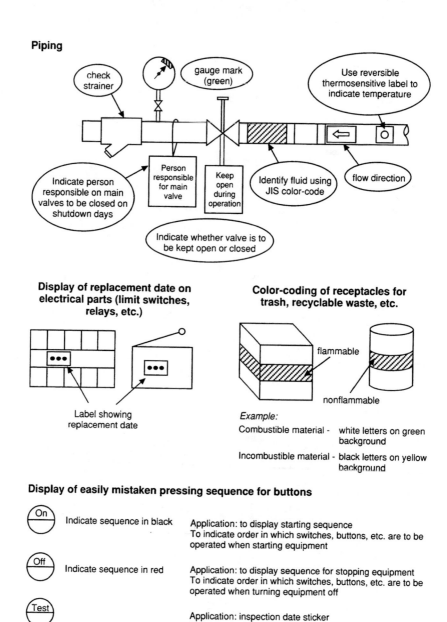

Display of replacement date on electrical parts (limit switches, relays, etc.)

Label showing replacement date

Color-coding of receptacles for trash, recyclable waste, etc.

flammable

nonflammable

Example:

Combustible material -   white letters on green background

Incombustible material - black letters on yellow background

Display of easily mistaken pressing sequence for buttons

On — Indicate sequence in black

Application: to display starting sequence
To indicate order in which switches, buttons, etc. are to be operated when starting equipment

Off — Indicate sequence in red

Application: to display sequence for stopping equipment
To indicate order in which switches, buttons, etc. are to be operated when turning equipment off

Test

Application: inspection date sticker
Record scheduled inspection date and affix to part to be inspected

Figure 3-21. Examples of Visual Controls

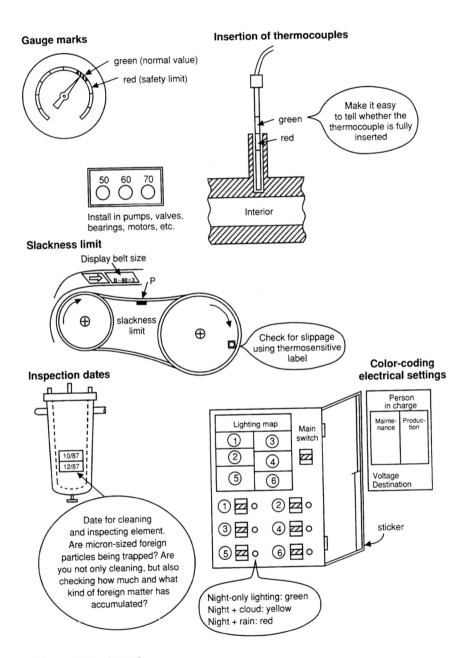

Figure 3-21. (cont.)

Some examples of general inspection elements follow (see Figure 3-22):

- Pneumatics: hoses, piping, FRLs (filter, regulator, and lubricator sets), pneumatic valves
- Hydraulics: hydraulic units, hydraulic cylinders, packing, strainers, filters
- Transmissions: couplings, chains, V-belts, speed reducers
- Electrical: limit switches, beam sensors, motors, thermocouples, level switches, control panels, wiring
- Containers: thermal insulation, coatings
- Measuring instruments: gauges, indicators, sensors
- Tooling: tools, dies, nipples, molds
- Drive systems: pumps, cooling towers, pump seals, float valves
- Liquids: cutting oil, hydraulic fluid
- Lubricants and mechanical elements: lubrication and tightening

Step 6: Seiri (Sorting Out) and Seiton (Arranging Efficiently)

Seiri (sorting out) consists of separating what is needed from what is not, and controlling the flow of things to prevent snags. Attach red picture cards to all items that have not been used for several months up to a year, and decide whether to scrap them. If nothing is done, things simply pile up. If you think of possible future uses, you will never throw anything out. Take the plunge and get rid of anything not actually in use.

To practice *seiton* (arranging efficiently), try to ensure that you can immediately lay your hands on the things you need in the necessary quantities at the right time and in good condition, without having to search for them. Decide where to place them and how to arrange them based on their frequency of use. Also decide who is responsible for looking after them from day to day and how they are to be replenished, scrapped, or otherwise disposed of. Seiton consists of developing the optimal layout for making the flow of things readily visible. It also consists of

Hydraulic units

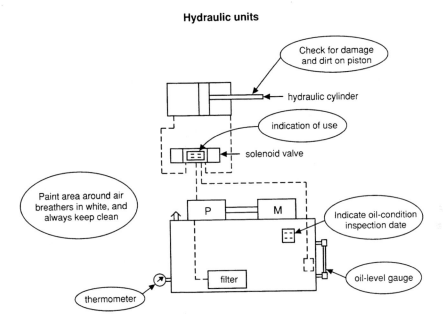

The four main enemies of hydraulic fluid

1. Air entrainment — no frothing.
2. Foreign matter (water, dust, foreign fluids) — clean air breathers, check filters, take care when changing fluid, inspect and clean fluid, etc.
3. High temperature — temperature should be below 55° C. Also be careful about differences in inlet and outlet fluid temperatures in heat exchangers.
4. Leaks — maintain packing and prevent vibration.

Surface damage to high-pressure hoses and wiring

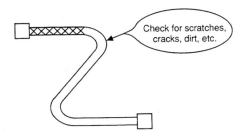

Figure 3-22. Example of General Inspection Items

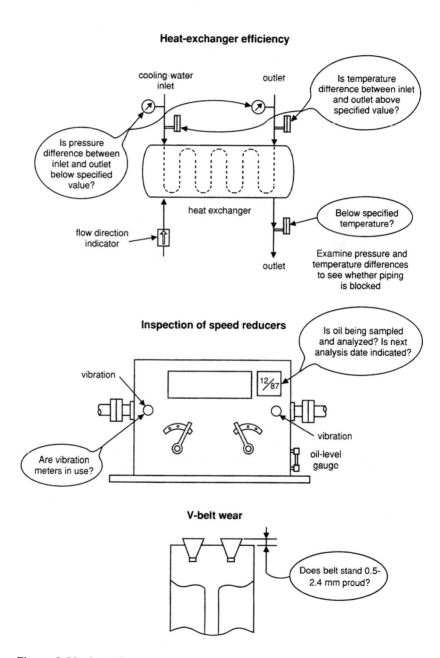

Figure 3-22. (cont.)

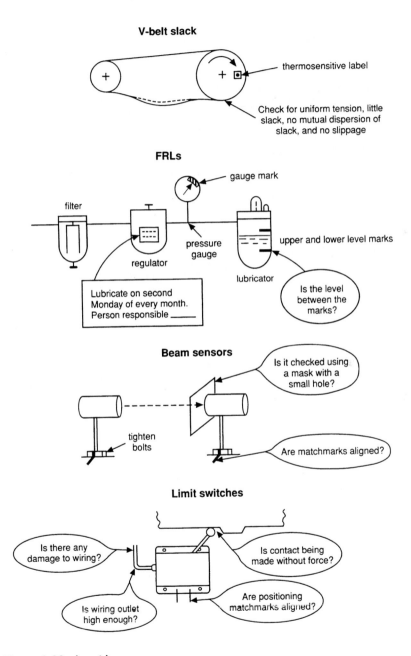

V-belt slack

thermosensitive label

Check for uniform tension, little slack, no mutual dispersion of slack, and no slippage

FRLs

gauge mark

filter

pressure gauge

regulator

upper and lower level marks

lubricator

Lubricate on second Monday of every month. Person responsible ____

Is the level between the marks?

Beam sensors

Is it checked using a mask with a small hole?

tighten bolts

Are matchmarks aligned?

Limit switches

Is there any damage to wiring?

Is contact being made without force?

Is wiring outlet high enough?

Are positioning matchmarks aligned?

Figure 3-22. (cont.)

studying changeover efficiency, and finding ways to standardize the layout to provide for good operability and easy maintenance. Things in constant use should be placed close at hand, things used occasionally should be kept in communal factory storage areas, and things used only rarely should be stored in warehouses.

The objects of seiri and seiton:

- Molds, dies, gauges, measuring instruments, jigs and tools, spare parts, fixtures, carts, cleaning tools, and other articles connected with failures and defects.
- Raw materials, work-in-process, completed products, surplus items, and dead stocks.

To reduce losses and eliminate defects, make it possible to tell at a glance whether the quality and quantity of things are as required. Do not take for granted the surplus items, dead stocks, and other debris cluttering your factory. Dispose of these, and take steps to prevent them from returning. Factories often make more items than ordered because they fear a certain percentage will be defective; the extra items are left lying around as surplus stock. Resolve from the start to never make more than the quantity ordered.

Rules for arranging things efficiently (see Figure 3-23) :

- Eliminate static electricity, dirt, rust, and other foreign matter. Methods could include placing items in vinyl bags or coating them with corrosion inhibitor.
- Arrange objects so that people will not bump into them.
- Label storage areas and indicate order point, order quantity, and procurement period. Simplify purchasing procedures by means of kanban* or cards, and move toward small-lot purchasing (see Figure 3-24).

---

* Kanban is a method of visual production control that uses a system of cards arranged on a board. As the level of cards with a particular reference number begins to rise, the need to resume production is immediately clear. For a more detailed description of the kanban method, refer to *The Visual Factory* by Michel Greif, Productivity Press, 1991.

Platforms

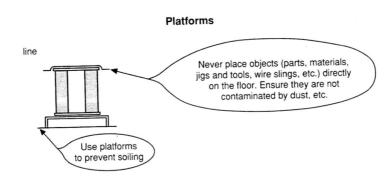

line

Never place objects (parts, materials, jigs and tools, wire slings, etc.) directly on the floor. Ensure they are not contaminated by dust, etc.

Use platforms to prevent soiling

Carts

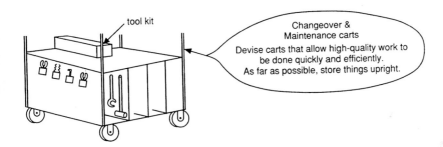

tool kit

Changeover & Maintenance carts
Devise carts that allow high-quality work to be done quickly and efficiently. As far as possible, store things upright.

Corner locators for storage areas

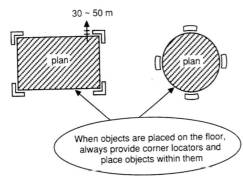

30 ~ 50 m

plan

plan

When objects are placed on the floor, always provide corner locators and place objects within them

Figure 3-23. Examples of Seiri and Seiton

**Wire
slings**

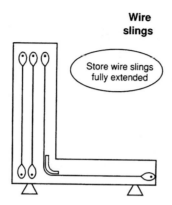

Store wire slings
fully extended

Examples of ideas for placing things

Place on pegs

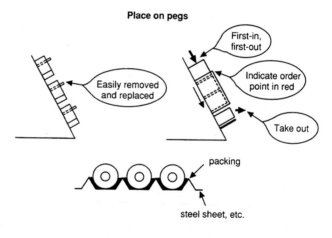

Easily removed
and replaced

First-in,
first-out

Indicate order
point in red

Take out

packing

steel sheet, etc.

No bumping

For small objects, use corrugated plastic sheet

Figure 3-23. (cont.)

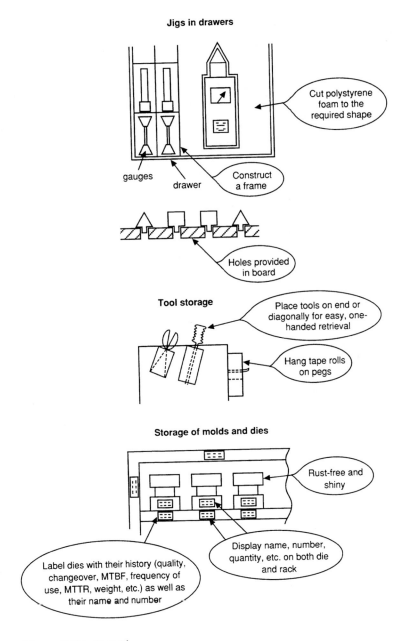

Jigs in drawers

Cut polystyrene foam to the required shape

gauges

drawer

Construct a frame

Holes provided in board

Tool storage

Place tools on end or diagonally for easy, one-handed retrieval

Hang tape rolls on pegs

Storage of molds and dies

Rust-free and shiny

Label dies with their history (quality, changeover, MTBF, frequency of use, MTTR, weight, etc.) as well as their name and number

Display name, number, quantity, etc. on both die and rack

Figure 3-23. (cont.)

Name	V-belt		Number	B-80	
Order point	Two		Order quantity	Four	
Supplier	Webster toolshop	Unit price	JY 588	Storage location	Power maintenance spare-part store
Average demand	6/month	Procure-ment lead time	1 day	Place of use	A 1 - 8 D 1 - 5
Past problems					
Stretching occurs if stored for too long					

Also describe past quality problems so anyone can see them at a glance

Figure 3-24. Spare-Part Kanban

- Arrange storage areas to facilitate transportation and to enable items to be stored and retrieved by the first-in, first-out method.
- Arrange things in straight lines, at right angles, vertically or in parallel.
- Mark receptacles and racks for defective items and surplus stocks in red.
- Never place things directly on the floor.
- Assign location numbers to storage areas.
- Stack vertically or diagonally rather than side-by-side.
- Write notices clearly.

Map-making: Find out the names, sizes, and places of use of all jigs and tools, then draw maps to help identify the most appropriate storage locations. Typical maps might include:

- Maps showing where jigs and tools are used, together with their names and sizes
- Maps of external setup points
- Defect maps

Step 7: Autonomous Inspection of Quality Components

At this step, staff help operators inspect quality components and add these procedures to the inspections they already perform. This is based on the inspection standards drawn up in Step 4 and is designed to lead to the development of effective autonomous quality inspection standards. The purpose is to enable operators to acquire the extra sensitivity they need to detect abnormalities quickly.

Previous steps made use of defects data and defects maps to show clearly what defects originate where. In addition, the equipment itself was carefully observed using drawings, catalogs, etc. As a result, the relation between the required quality characteristics and the equipment itself showed the exact locations of the quality components. In light of this knowledge, the autonomous inspection standards are revised, and inspection is carried out in accordance with them (see Figure 3-20).

The following items, together with those listed in Figure 3-25, are generally cited as examples of quality components, but these will differ depending on the particular equipment or type of product.

- Contact parts: guide rollers, spools, bearings, dies, molds
- Heating parts: heaters, thermocouples
- Cooling parts: hoses, pipes
- Transmission parts: couplings, rotating parts, belts, chains, brake shoes, sliding parts
- Work attachment parts: locators, chutes
- Fluids: filters, strainers, cutting oil, coolant
- Gauges and measuring instruments: mistake-proofing devices, calipers, gauges, thermometers, scales, etc.

No.	Quality component	Phenomenon	Preventive measure	Method of checking
	(Direct-type)			
1	Rollers	scratches, rust, wear, adhesion of foreign matter, soiling	clean	by touch
2	Spools	scratches, soiling, deformation, off-centering	handle with care	measure using gauges
3	Bearings	play, wear	lubricate	by stethoscope
4	Locators	displacement, slackness	tighten	matchmarks
5	Dies and molds	wear, corrosion, inaccuracy	accuracy control	dimensional measurement
6	Heaters	cutout	clean	measure current
7	Thermocouples	disconnection, removal	fix in position	visual check
8	Hoses and pipes	blockage, cracking	clean	measure flow rate
9	Couplings	play	tighten	check dimensions
10	Belts	slackness, wear	clean	measure slack
11	Chains	slackness, stretching	clean	measure tension
12	Brake shoes	wear	regular inspection	check dimensions
13	Chutes	blockage	regular inspection	visual check
14	Filters, strainers	blockage	regular inspection	pressure measurement
15	Presses and other machines	misalignment	accuracy control	measurement
16	Traversers	inaccurate movement	accuracy control	measurement
	(Indirect type) → cutting oil, coolant, air, and other fluids			
1	Dirt and foreign matter	blockage, surface damage	anti-source measures	check for dirty filters
2	Temperature	dispersion, temperature drop between inlet and outlet	regular inspection	measurement
3	Flow rate	blockage	regular inspection	visual check
4	Pressure	pumping-system abnormalities	regular inspection	visual check
5	Voltage, current	faulty contacts	regular inspection	visual check
6	Noise	disturbance	install shields	measure
7	Poles, slip rings	wear	regular inspection	measure

Figure 3-25. Direct and Indirect Quality Components

Step 8: Inculcation of Self-management

The aims of this step are to exploit the enthusiasm and skill generated in the previous steps in all aspects of the workplace and repeatedly maintain and improve the equipment while faithfully rotating the PDCA cycle. The importance of rotating the PDCA cycle has long been recognized, but it is easier to say than to do. At first, activity often came to a halt at the "plan" or "do" stage. Therefore, simplify the rotation of the PDCA cycle by the use of action-plan forms to ensure that people actually do the work rather than just talk about it or imagine they are doing it (see Figure 3-26).

These forms fulfill several functions. They serve to help determine and clarify work-team targets for PQCDSM (productivity, quality, cost, delivery, safety, and morale). Work teams use the forms to set their own quality targets as well as noting other matters and goals to be tackled, based on division and department managers' policies and objectives. These targets are not just result-oriented; they include effort-oriented targets that reveal whether people are really involved.

The forms also facilitate rotation of the PDCA cycle. They are used for planning daily maintenance management, improvements spanning periods of approximately one week, and for showing the priority topics for the month, all backed by sound rotation of the PDCA cycle. If problems occur, measures to prevent their recurrence, together with points for self-reflection, are noted in the "Special Remarks" column. This enables follow-up action to be carried out.

In addition, the forms provide support and encouragement from staff and superiors, and for this purpose a column is provided on the right-hand side. Superiors always record their opinions, impressions, and supportive remarks in this space at the end of each month, and use the forms to give appropriate support to supervisors during their daily rounds of the workplace.

The forms are also used at full briefing sessions held at the beginning of each month to report on the achievements of the

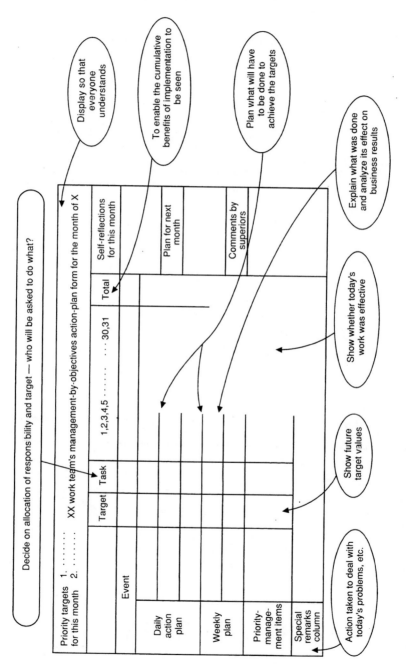

Figure 3-26. Key Points of Action-Plan Forms

previous one or two months and to follow up the rotation of the PDCA cycle. Naturally, staff also give their support at appropriate times.

To rotate the PDCA cycle properly, one has to become good with figures. It is all very well to visit the shop floor, but you will still overlook problems unless you have a grasp of the figures. Forgetting to bring the data with you is no excuse. Even in sports and games, top professionals make every effort to memorize the facts. Knowing the numbers and locations of the failures and defects that occurred the previous month enables you to check the current status by just looking at the workplace, and this leads to further improvements. It is impossible to check effectively unless you can at least remember details such as the number of limit switches on the equipment.

Benefits of a Certification System

The aim of combining the autonomous maintenance development steps with a certification system is to give participants a sense of achievement, let people know how fast or slow they are by competition and comparison with other groups, and accelerate overall progress. "Progress," in this sense, means lively and cheerful activity in a challenging atmosphere.

To decide on the levels to be accredited, start with a model line. Ensure that division and department managers thoroughly understand the actual situation in the workplace, then have them prepare certification checklists and other documents. Emphasize action and the spirit of challenge, since issuing certificates too readily or for halfhearted efforts will make the system a mere formality and will fail to foster real ability.

The roles of a certification system are:

- To clarify the level of achievement required at each accreditation step
- To make people strive toward the desired situation while efficiently rotating the PDCA cycle

- To raise the overall level of performance by intensifying the sense of competition
- To help to identify groups or teams that are slow and give them extra support

The type of certificate awarded should suit the situation in each workplace and may include the following:

- Five-S certificates (Class A, Class B)
- Autonomous maintenance certificates (various types)
- Quality maintenance certificates (various types) (see Figure 3-27)
- Productivity certificates (various types)
- Work-in-process reduction certificates (various types)
- Skill certificates (various types)

Maintenance Education and Training for Operators

To have the skilled labor required for practical autonomous maintenance and improvement activities, it is necessary to develop as many equipment-competent operators as possible. Merely teaching operators the minimum they need to know for routine operation and handling of their equipment does not give them the ability to make judgments or to effect improvements. It also means they will require more time to undertake new work and will tend to make frequent inadvertent errors.

If you want people to perform 10 actions reliably, teach them at least 20 or 30 items. In other words, give them not only *know-how* but also *know-why* to enable them to probe deeply into the mechanisms that make things happen. In terms of equipment, this means teaching them its functions and methods of construction. If they can understand these, they will capable of operating and manipulating equipment even more reliably.

Carry out practical education and training using autonomous maintenance manuals, one-point lessons and other materials. Actual equipment for the training is set up in areas on the shop floor (see Photo 3-1). Test trainees' understanding on

Class-B Autonomous Quality Maintenance Certificate Checklist for the Month of _____				
Group being audited	**X X X**		**Auditor**	**X X**
No.	**Check items**	**Standard**	**Score**	**Comments**
1	Exposure of minor flaws and defects by cleaning and inspection	5 or more per line	/3	
2	Initial cleaning	no dust, dirt, dead insects, etc.	/3	
3	Maps drawn showing sources of contamination, and countermeasures taken		/3	
4	Maps drawn showing places that are hard to inspect, and countermeasures taken		/3	
5	Pass-line cleaning and inspection		/3	
6	General quality inspection, education, and training	5 or more points	/3	
7	Improvement devices	"	/3	
8	Autonomous quality maintenance calendar (for maintenance during operation and during changeover)	implemented on own initiative	/3	
9	Maintenance and improvement based on MQP identification chart	application to chronic defects	/3	
10	Preparation and implementation of MQP cleaning and inspection standards	"	/3	
11	Control of dies and jigs	inspection on completion of use	/3	
12	Control of measuring instruments, sensors and mistake-proofing devices	self-management	/3	
13	Zero failures	0	/3	
14	Eradication of defects (major defects)	1/3 of defects	/3	
15	Planned quality maintenance	partial implementation	/3	
16	Quality maintenance self-reflection and study groups	2 or more one-point lessons	/3	
17	Skills stock-taking and education		/3	
18	Visual control	gauge marks, lubrication, thermosensitive labels	/3	
19	Limit samples		/3	
20	Defect recording and probing of causes		/3	
	Total		/60	

Figure 3-27. Example of Certification Checklist

completion of their training (see Figure 3-28), and award top
management certificates to those who master the requisite
maintenance skills (see Figure 3-29). To win these certificates,
people must fabricate actual pieces of work or effect specific
improvements. This kind of education gives even those who previously lacked interest in their equipment a great deal of satisfaction and the feeling that even they *can do it if they try*.

Some introductory topics for training include:

- Lubrication and tightening, FRLs, pneumatics, sensors,
  and other mechanical elements for general inspection
- Welding, cutting, drilling, plumbing, and other improvement skills
- Mechanisms of equipment failure components
- Sketching and drawing
- Minor repairs and servicing — skills such as installing
  keys and repairing damage to shafts. Teach the *know-why*
  — explaining, for example, "this is what will happen if
  the parts are not fitted to an accuracy of 1/100 mm."

Photo 3-1. Practical Training Using Actual Objects

The following five types of limit switch are those most commonly used.
Select the correct name for each from the list below and write its letter in the brackets.

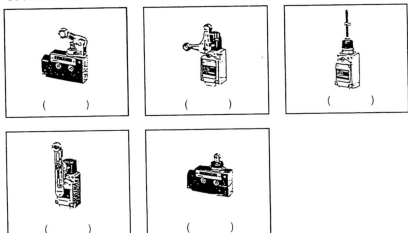

Names:
  a) Roller-flange type
  b) Roller-arm-lever type
  c) Coil-spring type
  d) Forked-lever rocking type
  e) Roller-lever type

Select the correct parts names and record them in the brackets on the diagram below.

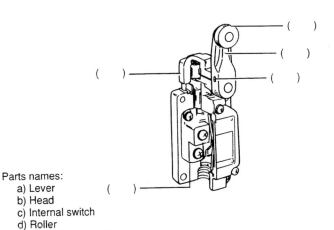

Parts names:
  a) Lever   (   )
  b) Head
  c) Internal switch
  d) Roller
  e) Roller-lever retaining screw

Figure 3-28. Test of Understanding

Start date: Year   Month   Day   Equipment name   Instructor

Operator Skills Check Sheet   Name and work team

	Category	Key point	Skill mastered O	△	×
Step 1		Knows checklist and inspection points accurately			
		Can report, liaise, and describe properly			
		Can select inspection method and judge whether or not abnormality is present			
		Possesses simple skills such as lubrication adjustment			
	Regular inspection and servicing (mechanical)	Can replace guide rollers and bearings (can check centering)			
	Masters skills by working with maintenance personnel	Can assess belt wear, replace, and adjust belts			
		Can assess roller-chain wear, replace, adjust, and lubricate			
	Takes positive steps to learn by doing (through familiarization rather than being taught)	Can dismantle and clean speed-reducer oil filters and check oil contamination			
		Can check adjustment screws as well as pulley and sprocket keys			
	Acquires the ability to judge what is and is not an abnormality	Can repair leaks (oil, water, air) and tighten pump connections			
		Can replace brakes and torque reducers			
	What is wear?	Can replace and center joints, bolts, chains, tires, etc.			
	What is adjustment?	Can check operation of replacement parts			

Step 2	Regular inspection and maintenance (electrical) — is not afraid of electricity and realizes that there is no danger if one knows the basic rules and follows them	Replace indicator light, replace lighting, clean work tools
		Can tighten and adjust slackness in limit switches and proximity switches
		Can adjust position, tighten, and clean beam sensors
	Acquisition of ability to judge abnormalities	Can perform operation checks
		Can clean, adjust, replace, and service motor brushes
	• What is a malfunction?	Can test insulation and clean slip rings
	• What is brush wear?	Can tighten control knobs and zero gauges
	Minor repair work (action to deal with sudden failures)	Can center and replace belts and pulleys on tachometer-generators
		Can perform emergency splicing and taping of damaged cables
Step 3		Can replace guide-roller bearings, belts, traversing hooks, drum rings, bobbin cones, retaining screws, snap bolts, grease nipples, FRLs, brakes, fuses, caps, etc.

Note: When filling out the *skill mastered* columns, the instructor should record the date in the upper boxes and sign the lower boxes

Figure 3-29. Maintenance Skills Check Sheet

Training by Maintenance Personnel

As part of their responsibilities, maintenance personnel must train equipment operators in maintenance techniques. It is no longer enough just to be a maintenance or repair person. As many learning opportunities as possible must be created for operators. For example, maintenance personnel should always invite operators to visit the repair shop and lend a hand with maintenance work. When doing their rounds, maintenance personnel should check how operators perform their daily inspections. Operators should ask what has happened when a breakdown occurs or equipment has been restored. Operators should learn about their equipment by helping with breakdown repairs and planned maintenance work.

By these and other means, support is given to the attitude that operators should make a positive effort to learn from maintenance personnel.

One-point Lessons

The most obvious details are often not communicated and not understood. The value of one-point lessons lies in the fact that anybody can prepare them and use them to teach others rapidly at any time. One-point lesson sheets are regularly used to check people's level of understanding. Excellent results can be obtained if quotas are set and hundreds or thousands of one-point lesson sheets are prepared for use (see Photo 3-2; Figure 3-30).

Learning Equipment Names

The development of equipment consciousness and autonomous maintenance starts with a study of the names of equipment components. If a machine fails and the operator does not know the name of the broken component, he or she will be unable to give the necessary information to the mainte-

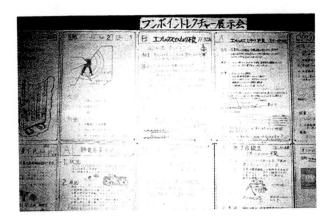

Photo 3-2. One-Point Lesson Sheet

nance department over the telephone. The maintenance person will then have to come to the shop floor to check before returning to collect the replacement part. However, if the operator knows the name of the part, information can be given over the telephone and the time needed for restoring the equipment can be greatly reduced.

Although it is a good idea to mark each piece of equipment with its name, model and size so that anyone can see this information at a glance, this is not all that is required by way of education (see Figure 3-31). Operators should be made to memorize the names of the components of their equipment, either in the training area or the classroom, using either the equipment itself or cutaway models (see Photo 3-3).

This chapter has described the development and inculcation of daily self-management activities through implementation of the Five S's, autonomous maintenance, and visual controls as the preparatory conditions for MQP management. The important effect is the degree to which these activities change everybody's behavior.

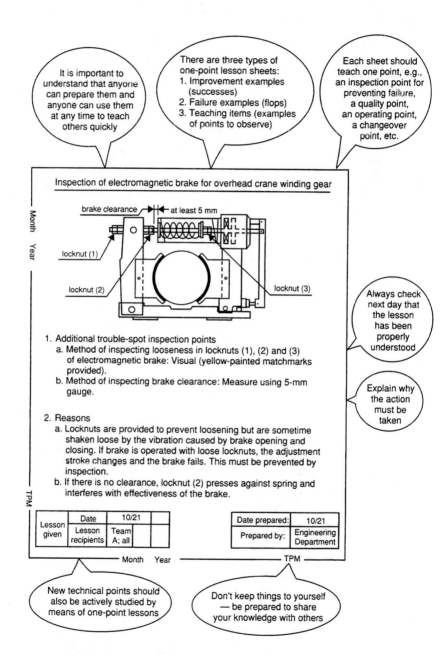

It is important to understand that anyone can prepare them and anyone can use them at any time to teach others quickly

There are three types of one-point lesson sheets:
1. Improvement examples (successes)
2. Failure examples (flops)
3. Teaching items (examples of points to observe)

Each sheet should teach one point, e.g., an inspection point for preventing failure, a quality point, an operating point, a changeover point, etc.

Inspection of electromagnetic brake for overhead crane winding gear

brake clearance — at least 5 mm

locknut (1)

locknut (2)

locknut (3)

Month Year

TPM

Always check next day that the lesson has been properly understood

Explain why the action must be taken

1. Additional trouble-spot inspection points
   a. Method of inspecting looseness in locknuts (1), (2) and (3) of electromagnetic brake: Visual (yellow-painted matchmarks provided).
   b. Method of inspecting brake clearance: Measure using 5-mm gauge.

2. Reasons
   a. Locknuts are provided to prevent loosening but are sometime shaken loose by the vibration caused by brake opening and closing. If brake is operated with loose locknuts, the adjustment stroke changes and the brake fails. This must be prevented by inspection.
   b. If there is no clearance, locknut (2) presses against spring and interferes with effectiveness of the brake.

| Lesson given | Date | 10/21 | | | Date prepared: | 10/21 |
| | Lesson recipients | Team A; all | | | Prepared by: | Engineering Department |

Month Year ———— TPM

New technical points should also be actively studied by means of one-point lessons

Don't keep things to yourself — be prepared to share your knowledge with others

Figure 3-30. One-Point Lesson Sheet

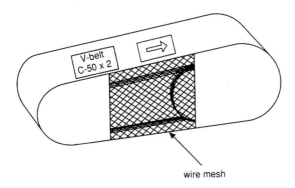

wire mesh

Figure 3-31. Indicate Belt Size on Safety Cover

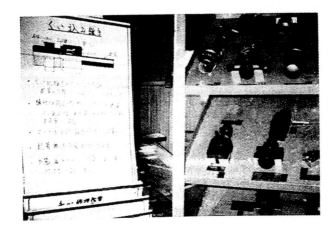

Photo 3-3. Cutaway Models in the Training Area

4

The Mechanisms Behind
Failures and Defects

This chapter discusses the equipment mechanisms that are operating when failures and defects occur. This understanding is essential to the development of MQP management.

EQUIPMENT-ORIGINATED DEFECTS

Equipment failures fall into one of two categories:

- The type of failure that causes cessation of a function (stoppage failure)
- The type of failure that affects quality or causes functional deterioration (deterioration failure)

With deterioration failure, the equipment does not stop working, but inaccuracies and other types of functional deterioration create equipment-originated defects. MQP management is a system for eliminating this type of failure. In the past, production and maintenance departments worried only about stoppage failure, and were uninterested in deterioration failure. This meant that, when equipment-originated defects occurred, both departments simply blamed the equipment. Countermeasures were seldom effected.

As described in the previous chapters, however, the concern now is with the type of failure that affects quality or causes functional deterioration. It is necessary to promote activities aimed at preventing this deterioration by eliminating minor flaws. These activities are based on an understanding of the underlying mechanisms that generate this particular type of failure.

THE TYPICAL FAILURE-RATE CURVE

It was once thought that new equipment would inevitably pass through a stage in which many failures occur (called the *early failure period*), while old equipment would become decrepit after a time and therefore be less reliable (the *wear-out failure period*). However, by involving the production and maintenance departments from the design stage, practicing *early equipment management* (management of the transition from installation to normal production), and striving to build highly reliable equipment, it is possible to achieve smooth startup of new equipment and severely curtail the early failure period.

Activities aimed at measuring and preventing deterioration can also lower the failure-rate curve by eliminating failures during the random-failure period. Careful maintenance has also been very successful in preventing the failure rate from rising in the wear-out failure period. This is achieved by replacing deteriorated and worn-out parts early and restoring the equipment to perfect condition.

Although it is impossible to prevent equipment from becoming obsolete, the development of TPM and MQP allow you to use common sense and ingenuity to limit the effects of its deterioration at every stage of the equipment operating life. This enables you to improve failure rate levels beyond those previously considered possible (see Figure 4-1).

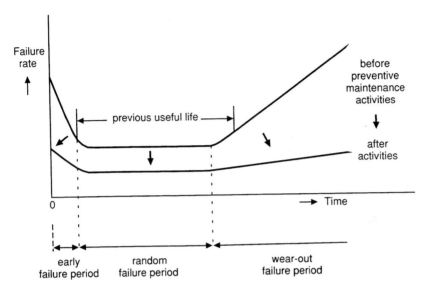

Figure 4-1. The Typical Failure-Rate Curve (Bathtub Curve)

EQUIPMENT DETERIORATION

Refer to Figure 4-2. The strength distribution is quite high at point $t = 0$. However, as time passes, equipment components are subject to accelerated deterioration as a result of dirt and other factors, in addition to natural deterioration. Equipment strength therefore decreases with time.

Meanwhile, stresses on machined components also tend to increase as a result of worsening environmental conditions and other factors. When the strength and stress distributions overlap (as at point t_1), failures or defects occur as a result of breakage, wear, or other types of deterioration. It is, therefore, important to prevent both accelerated deterioration and any worsening of environmental conditions.

With stoppage failures, it is obvious when the failure point (point t_1 in Figure 4-2) has been reached. The equipment stops

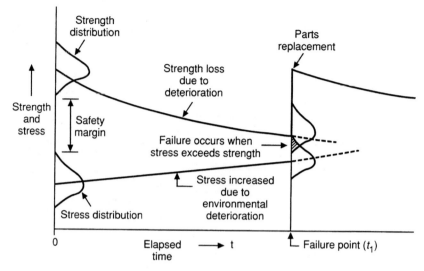

Figure 4-2. Equipment Deterioration

working. With deterioration failures, however, it is often difficult to measure this point. Nevertheless, the philosophy of PM
is to predict this point and take preventive action before it is
reached. Strengthen your deterioration-measuring activities to
enable you to replace parts before point t_1 is reached, restoring
equipment to its optimal condition and maintaining it in that
state. It is important when replacing components to measure
their degree of deterioration and to use this data for deciding
when to do the next replacement.

It is generally claimed that the life of control panel components will be halved for each 10 degrees Celsius the temperature
of the interior rises above the normal. Also, the life of a machine
is said to decrease in proportion to the square of the factor by
which its speed is increased, and the failure frequency will increase correspondingly. Before you increase rotation speeds,
therefore, eliminate any existing sources of accelerated deterioration and strengthen any mechanically weak areas.

OUTMODED THINKING AND EQUIPMENT FAILURES

Equipment failures can be eliminated through universal implementation of maintenance measures such as measuring deterioration and eliminating accelerated deterioration. However, some people throw in the towel and abandon PM as soon as equipment grows old, thinking that, because of its age, it is bound to break down. But, as previously explained, it is possible to restore even old equipment to its original condition by the thorough application of PM. If failures and defects do not decrease, it is not because the equipment is old but because people's thinking is out-of-date. Two causes of failures are not noticing that dirt and other factors are accelerating the deterioration (accelerated deterioration), and not noticing the deterioration itself (failing to check).

The following six items can generally be cited as causes of frequent failures (see Figure 4-3):

- Dirt, blockages, surface damage, and foreign matter: these can be prevented by cleaning, eliminating the sources of contamination, stopping the scattering of debris, and by pressure measurement
- Improper lubrication: prevented by daily lubrication, and measurement of heat generation and vibration
- Excessive play and leakage due to looseness of parts: prevented by regular tightening, and checking of match-marks
- Wear and corrosion: detected by measurements using thickness and contour gauges, vibration meters, etc.
- Breakage and fatigue: detected visually and by stress analysis
- Deformation and warping: prevented by control of accuracy

Since these types of failure phenomena are easy to check and spot through measurement and other activities, it is well worth the effort to prevent them from happening in the first

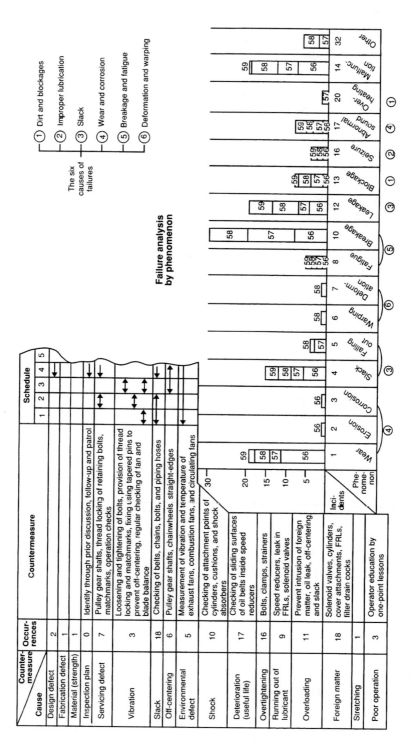

Figure 4-3. Cause Analysis and Countermeasure Schedule for Sheet Line

place. Whether failures occur or are eliminated depends wholly on the way people think and behave.

MULTIPLE CAUSES OF FAILURES AND DEFECTS

Chronic failures and chronic equipment-originated defects rarely have a single cause, but are due to the interplay of large numbers of minor flaws and malfunctions. Because of the large number of them, it is often impossible to identify each one conclusively as a cause. It is not usually very effective to label only one or two as causes and take action only against these; however, improvements will never happen if you adopt the attitude that nothing can be done unless *all* the causes are known. The difficulty of establishing a cause-and-effect relationship is a characteristic of minor flaws. Dealing with minor flaws and malfunctions is hindered in the following cases:

- When the minor flaws and malfunctions themselves cannot be found
- When, even though they are known to exist, they are randomly dispersed and are not thought to be causes
- When, even though their dispersion is recognized, they are ignored because they are thought to be of no consequence
- When minor flaws are ignored and no action is attempted until a definite cause is found

To eliminate failures and defects, it is necessary to discover and take preventive action against all minor flaws and malfunctions even when they are thought to have little or no relation to the problem at hand.

ACTIVITIES TO PREVENT DETERIORATION

To eliminate failures and defects, focus your effort on activities to prevent deterioration. If equipment breaks down at night when there are no maintenance technicians present, you could telephone technicians at home and call them out, and have everyone try to restore the equipment to working order promptly. However, activities to prevent deterioration are far more effective, yet tend to be ignored. Leaving all PM activities to an elite squad of maintenance technicians is not very effective. The person who actually operates a machine is in the best position to assess its condition, and success can be achieved by giving operators the main role in preventing deterioration. Operators cannot look after every aspect of their equipment, but with the help of maintenance technicians, they can do much to prevent its deterioration. These activities can be promoted by making maintenance personnel responsible for teaching operators and having the two departments work together while fulfilling their individual roles, as shown in Figure 4-4.

This chapter has stressed that it is the plethora of easily overlooked minor flaws that causes defects by accelerating equipment deterioration. These flaws must be brought to light even if the cause-and-effect relationships are unknown. The operators' role in this is vital.

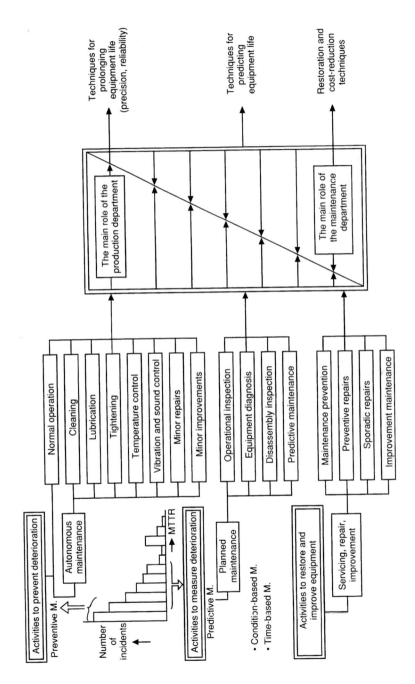

Figure 4-4. Share of Maintenance Tasks Between Production and Maintenance

5

The Basic Approach to
Defect Prevention

This chapter describes the ten-point approach required for developing MQP management. The most important feature is that everybody from top executives to shop-floor workers must play a part. Everyone in every relevant division must take up the challenge of quality-oriented TPM (i.e., MQP management), not just the maintenance division, but also the production, production engineering, quality assurance, technical, and other divisions.

There must be a common striving toward the target of zero defects by treating the equipment (machines, jigs, tools, molds, dies, measuring instruments, and so on) with interest and concern, and by dealing promptly with minor equipment flaws. Total productive maintenance is a vital issue that all employees must unite to address.

Maintenance people should have production figures such as output operating rates, defect rates, and loss rates at their fingertips, while operators and production staff should be knowledgeable about their equipment and conversant with productive maintenance. Quality assurance department staff should take an interest in any equipment that creates defects, and equipment designers must design new equipment that is reliable and easy to use.

It is wrong to leave everything up to the production line; all relevant staff divisions should also concern themselves with the equipment. They should consider ways of supporting and assisting the shop-floor personnel as they deal with complex problems, and find the best ways to help people on the front line of production. Top management's role is to demonstrate their interest and concern, make policies, set up promotional systems, and sponsor improvement activities (see Figure 5-1).

Division and department managers must clarify TPM policy, objectives, and measures. Then, based on these, they must set specific goals and policies for individual work teams and product lines, as well as provide regular guidance and follow-up. They should also understand equipment better than anyone else so that they can lead their subordinates. In many cases, it will be necessary for them to perform their own share of the Five-S work.

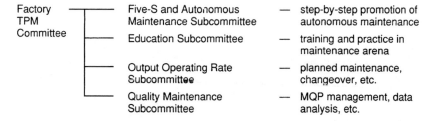

Figure 5-1. The TPM Promotion Organization

THE ROLE OF SHOP-FLOOR WORKERS

In an old-fashioned production plant, it was thought sufficient for workers simply to make things in accordance with standards and instructions issued by staff. Today, however, the shop floor must take the lead for building in quality through the process. Shop-floor workers must be resolute and ask themselves, "If we don't take up the zero-defect challenge, who will?" The amount of effort the shop floor puts into maintenance and improvement thus becomes a vital issue. As many people as possible must be trained to know their equipment well, maintain and improve it themselves by observing what is actually happening on the spot, and feel responsible for looking after their own equipment and processes. In this way, much more self-reliant workplaces can be developed.

Shop-floor workers must discover the best way to look after the areas for which they are responsible, and the best way to change the things that need changing. A factory can never be called top-rank if it has a weak shop floor, and to make it stronger demands the wisdom and ingenuity not of one person but of many.

Against this background, the role of shop-floor managers and supervisors is to make high-quality products cheaply, at the right time, and in the right quantities, with the equipment and staffing allocated. To achieve this, they have to make things better today than yesterday, and better tomorrow than today. They must realize that their job is not just *making* things, but *changing* things. They need to understand and do a great many tasks. They must know what the people under them are doing, be able to show them how to do the work, and, by trying the job for themselves, discover hidden waste. They must take the lead and set an example in locating and eliminating hidden losses and waste on the shop floor.

The level of enthusiasm with which routine shop-floor activities are performed, such as autonomous maintenance, autonomous inspection, circle activities, and suggestion schemes, is a reliable indicator of whether the shop floor has autonomy and initiative.

THE TRANSPARENT WORKPLACE

On any shop floor, there are many checks to be performed and many tasks to be done. A lot of these are not at all obvious, and this is why the system of visual control was introduced. Its aim is to enable more people to become involved in shop-floor tasks, and its three main objectives are:

1. To allow efficient monitoring of large numbers of potential causes of defects
2. To enable more people to participate in maintenance and improvement
3. To encourage hands-on activity rather than discussion

To achieve these objectives, visual control attempts to make obvious to all what is happening in the workplace and to indicate what is clearly normal and what is abnormal. It allows division and department managers to take the lead and set an example.

When one pair of eyes is not enough to check for equipment abnormalities and minor flaws, it is important to inspect and verify with two pairs or more. To achieve this, make it possible to tell by just looking at the workplace whether the appropriate checks have been performed and when the next ones are due. Preparing reams of beautiful checklists and covering them with check marks does not help morale if defects persist.

Some types of visual controls are as follows (see Figure 5-2):

- Displays on equipment — important operating and control points, operation and inspection status, and so on
- Management-by-objectives board — tackling of objectives, details of activity development, and so on
- Displays on people — qualification badges on helmets, and so on
- Displays on raw materials, work-in-process and completed products — scheduled and actual processing dates, and so on

THE IMPORTANCE OF IDENTIFYING CAUSES

It has always been very important to use control charts and other statistical tools to analyze failure and defects data and phe-

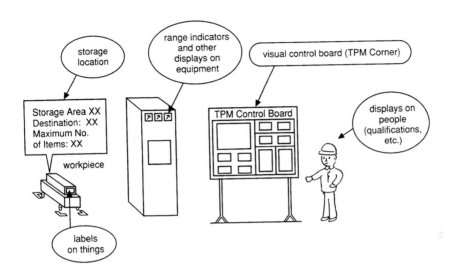

Figure 5-2. Visual Controls

nomena, and to identify their causes. People are generally interested in using defects data to discover why and how defects occur; and countermeasures are often implemented only after data analysis has shown certain specific causes to be significant.

However, equipment-originated defects often have a great many intertwined causal factors, making it impossible to pin down specific causes at the initial stage of analysis. Even when data analysis is performed, it frequently happens that little of significance is found and the causes cannot be identified. This is particularly true when attention is focused on result data, and few observations or measurements are performed on processing conditions and equipment. If the true causes cannot be found, adequate measures will not be taken to prevent recurrence of the problem (see Figure 5-3).

Before spending much time and effort on analyzing defect data (i.e., result data) to discover and prove what the causes are, it is better to go to the workplace and examine all factors suspected of being possible causes, look at how they are dispersed, and take the practical approach of maintaining them in their ideal condition.

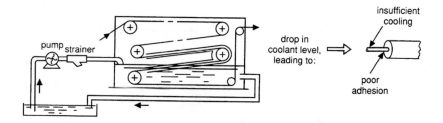

1. Poor adhesion — cause unknown — for fear of recurrence, cause investigated by on-the-spot experiment to recreate the defect

2. Cause finally identified by experiment — beautiful report prepared

3. Having identified cause, experimenters rest on their laurels — equipment or other department blamed, but no action taken

4. Cooling system inadequately maintained — nothing done to make coolant level visible

5. Summary — engineers tend to zero in on a single cause
   - They are only interested in analyzing the failure, not in taking steps to prevent it
   - Most of the work-hours used by the production engineering division are spent on corrective action (shutting the gate after the horse has bolted)
   - Preemptive control appears at first glance to require more labor, but is easier in the long run

Figure 5-3. Conventional Defect Countermeasures

Statistical tools. The use of statistical tools should not be confined to analyzing data on results alone; they should also be used extensively to analyze measurement data at the cause end of the cause-and-effect chain and to plot how the causes themselves change.

Maintenance analysis. If a failure or a defect occurs, a failure analysis should be performed to find out what happened. But this is not all. A maintenance analysis should also be performed to analyze people's behavior and to answer questions such as "Why was the failure not detected before it happened?" "Was it a component that had been ignored?" and "Could the failure have been detected before it happened?" (see Figure 5-4). If the cause turns out to be something that had been neglected, then serious self-examination is required.

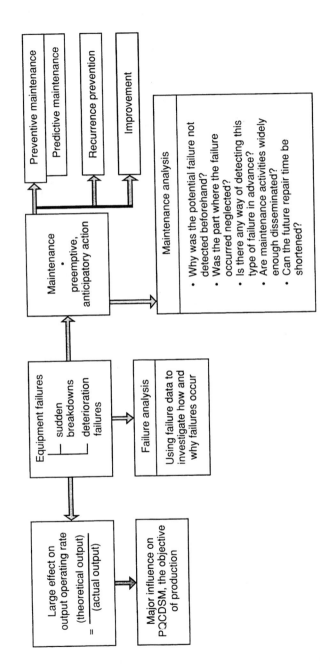

Figure 5-4. Failure Analysis and Maintenance Analysis

Shutdown conditions. In pursuing the ideal processing and equipment conditions (i.e., the causes), people are often concerned solely with ensuring that the equipment is in proper condition when it is started up. They overlook important information in failing to check its condition when it is shut down after use. Since equipment deteriorates, checks should be made at shutdown to ensure that it is still within the tolerance limits and has not changed from its optimal state. In other words, all's well that ends well.

THE IMPORTANCE OF PREVENTION AND MAINTENANCE

When a failure or defect occurs in most factories, the usual procedure is to find out how it happened and what caused it, then to instigate measures designed to prevent it from recurring. Although such measures may reduce trouble temporarily, they cannot eliminate defects in the long term. The proof of this is that many factories are unable to reduce the number of failures, defects, and minor stoppages even though cause-and-effect diagrams are prepared and the appropriate actions are taken. The countermeasures employed are often inadequate, failing to reach the true causes or addressing only some of them. Also, operators are often good at performing daily inspections using checklists and making lots of check marks, but poor at maintenance and standardization.

Prevention means taking action to stop something from happening. To achieve this, you must strive to identify all processing conditions and components which could possibly cause defects, continually monitor and uncover variations and abnormalities in these (i.e., minor flaws), and take action to prevent them from developing into defects. Aim to abolish defects entirely by refining this procedure until you eliminate any possibility of defects occurring in the first place. As a method of attack, it is one step ahead of recurrence prevention (see Figure 5-5).

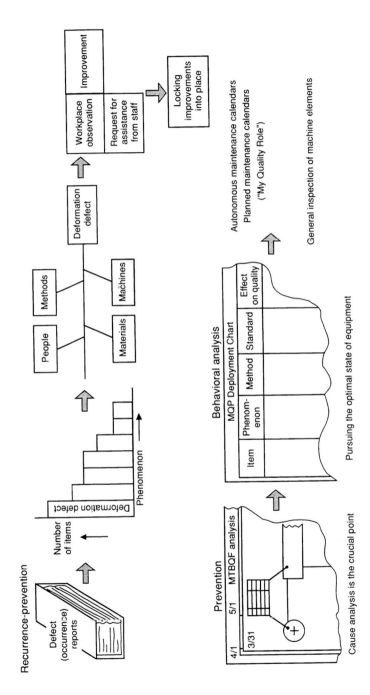

Figure 5-5. Failure Elimination and the Use of Control Data

Again, maintenance divisions are generally disinterested in quality, while production divisions are indifferent about equipment. This means that the type of equipment failure that leads to functional deterioration and results in quality defects and quality-related minor stoppages is usually neglected. In the past, prevention activities were not usually directed at failures related to quality. MQP management extends the theory and practice of prevention and maintenance to include quality problems.

However, in developing the concept of prevention and making it second nature, you must take preemptive action against potential causes of trouble before knowing for certain that they will lead to problems. This requires no ordinary zeal. It takes great persistence and a willingness to proceed inexorably one step at a time by laying down rules for behavior and accumulating a succession of small improvements. It is important to realize from the start that it is no "quick fix," and that halfhearted promotion measures are doomed to failure. Prevention and maintenance are impossible without belief, commitment, and persistence.

Once a prevention system has been established, people will be constantly aware of the possible causes of failures and defects. If trouble does occur, they will soon know the likely group of causes and will be able to take the measures necessary to prevent a recurrence.

IMPROVEMENT PRIORITIES

Improvements aimed at eliminating failures and defects are of two types: hardware (equipment) improvements and managerial/educational improvements. Hardware improvements are those that strengthen or modify failed parts. Managerial and educational improvements are operational and behavioral improvements such as the Five S's, autonomous maintenance, one-point lessons, establishment of standard procedures, and so on.

The best kind of improvement is one that costs nothing and yields the optimum results. Divisions that concentrate all their efforts on hardware improvements with a small team of staff find that, even when failures and defects decrease, the decrease is only temporary.

MQP management, on the other hand, is based on ensuring that people lay down the rules and then follow them conscientiously, without necessarily spending money for hardware improvements. It gives managerial and educational improvements priority over hardware improvements, yielding significant benefits. It not only permits the elimination of equipment-originated causes of defects and failures, but it also inculcates basic skills, reduces careless mistakes, and awakens people to a sense of responsibility (see Figure 5-6).

IMPLEMENTING IMPROVEMENTS

Even when many problems are identified and plenty of improvement suggestions are made through workplace observation and measurement, people often have trouble with the next step: implementation. Reasons for this include the inability to decide on the specific details of an improvement or, having decided them, taking too long to turn them into reality. This reveals a lack of improvement ability. What is needed are people who are interested in and understand their equipment, are well-versed in specific technologies and equipment technology, and who have accumulated enough experience to put improvement suggestions into effect speedily. It is even more desirable for people to make their own improvement suggestions and put them into effect themselves.

There are unlimited opportunities for people to improve their abilities if they want to. They can do this by going to maintenance school to improve their kaizen abilities, by joining equipment-improvement teams and taking positive action, and by setting up improvement teams in the workplace and obtaining practical experience.

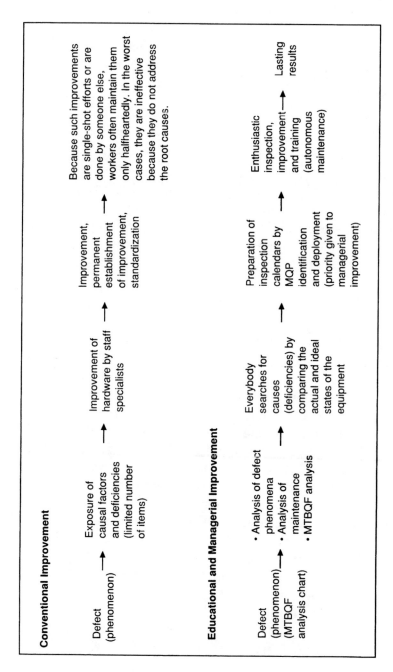

Figure 5-6. The Difference Between Conventional Improvement Promotion and Managerial Improvement Promotion

When there is nobody capable of making improvements, maintenance people are often used merely as handymen and are employed in simple fabrication tasks. But this erodes their ability to perform preventive maintenance. People must no longer be divided into production and maintenance camps. It is vitally important to have as many people as possible who know their equipment well, can put forward improvement suggestions, and can translate their ideas into reality.

IDENTIFYING LOSS AND WASTE

Financial losses due to failures and defects are usually calculated on the basis of their effect on direct costs such as labor, subcontracting, energy consumption, maintenance expenses, material costs, etc. However, the hidden indirect losses actually far exceed these. The reason they stay hidden is that many people think defects are inevitable and fail to notice the magnitude of the losses they create. To make everybody realize the full impact of defects, start by having people express defects as much as possible in the form of numbers or financial loss.

Some problems related to finding hidden losses are:

- When many serious failures and defects occur, it is difficult to deal with small, concealed defects and quality-related idling and minor stoppages, and the losses due to these are overlooked.
- Little attention is paid to rework or to the material losses that result when materials are handled and measured. These losses are due to ignorance and a lack of creative ideas, so do not be deluded into thinking that many of them are inevitable for technical reasons.
- People are unable to leave equipment unattended during operation for fear that something might go wrong.
- When failures and defects occur, production control staff have to rush around trying to ensure that delivery dates

are met, and much time is wasted interacting with sales staff and customers.

- Vast amounts of time and effort are expended in dealing with customer complaints about defects.
- Surplus items and dead stocks accumulate as a result of making extra products as a safety margin in case some of the production is defective.

ACHIEVING PRACTICAL BENEFITS

Acting in accordance with the needs and aims of the various divisions is a precondition of MQP management as well as other management systems, and will lead to practical advantages. It is particularly important to recognize the value and benefit of total participation activities and equipment improvements, and to promote these harmoniously based on needs (see Figure 5-7).

Surprisingly, the Five S's often make a factory spotless on the surface but fail to penetrate to the key areas affecting quality and productivity. MQP management goes beyond superficial "Environmental Five S's," evolving into "Quality Five S's" and autonomous quality maintenance with goals based on true needs, and it has beneficial effects on factory business management.

There is a big gap between understanding something and doing something about it. Without considerable resolve, people will not move from the *thinking* stage to the *doing* stage. Even

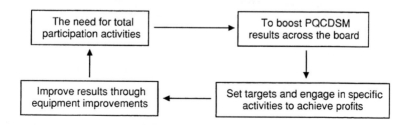

Figure 5-7. Total Participation Activities and Equipment Improvements

when they recognize the need for action and are willing to make a move, the circumstances must make action possible. When the action stage is reached, time, space, and materials are needed — and division and department managers must take positive steps to supply these. However, managers must not simply pressure their subordinates into acting and leave things up to them; they must show leadership qualities. All too often, division and department managers do not show their subordinates how to act, do not make the necessary decisions or allocate roles and responsibilities, and do not give their subordinates enough time. However, if managers exercise leadership, then improvements occur quickly, wrong methods are used less often, and the benefits accumulate rapidly.

Managers must have the courage and initiative to achieve targets faster and do more than outside consultants advise. They must set policies and objectives for activities, make plans, decide their roles, and rotate the PDCA cycle to increase their capacity to understand, plan, measure, analyze, execute, improve, and judge. The degree to which division and department managers develop these abilities with commitment and persistence will determine the strength and success of their divisions and the company as a whole.

6

MQP Management through Equipment Improvement

This chapter discusses the deployment of MQP management through equipment improvement. It assumes that both autonomous quality maintenance and the basic philosophy discussed in the previous chapters are in place. In MQP management, you start with an equipment improvement and build it into a routine control procedure by reviewing autonomous maintenance and similar activities.

Defect countermeasures devised by the standing organization or small groups as part of routine control and autonomous maintenance activities usually succeed in solving the basic problems that are tackled. In certain areas, however, eliminating defects completely can take months if this is the only method used. This is why, for pressing problems requiring immediate results and for problems that are difficult to solve through the permanent TPM organization or small-group activities, the deployment of MQP management through equipment improvement must be encouraged.

This chapter describes the goals of MQP management through equipment improvement and explains how it is promoted. Its deployment often pushes improvements through at previously unheard-of speeds and yields impressive results.

THE IMPROVEMENT SESSION

A manufacturing division may face problems that it is eager to solve even if it means calling for outside help. This division defines the topic, sets the goals and provides an arena in which members of an equipment-improvement team drawn from other divisions can hold a whirlwind one-day session during which they bring all their respective specialty skills to bear on finding an urgent solution. Besides achieving the specified goals and having a powerful impact on the division that provides this training ground, a further benefit of this exercise is that it enables the participants to increase their improvement abilities as a result of the team effort.

This approach can be used not only for tackling defects but also for reducing material losses and devising countermeasures against idling and minor stoppages even when their causes are unclear, and it produces excellent results.

The Role of Division and Section Managers

A small improvement team is formed with the participation of division and section managers from other divisions, such as manufacturing, quality assurance, production technology, maintenance, and equipment design. In principle, the goal of MQP management through equipment improvements is to have the improvement team, headed by division and section managers, take a single day to achieve the targets relating to the topic set by the division providing the problem-solving arena, or else devise a plan or suggestion for improvement. This type of improvement session is designed for tackling specific topics with high targets such as eliminating defects or cutting losses in half. This is accomplished by deliberately creating a situation in which everyone must cheerfully and energetically pool their knowledge and ideas and exercise their abilities in an intense burst. Their goal is to complete the improvement in one day. It lets division and section managers show what they can do rather than just give orders, and it allows them to develop their own improvement abilities and exercise their leadership in a practical way.

Preparation

Before a division requests an equipment improvement session, it must, of course, have done everything possible through autonomous maintenance and other routine control activities. The more extensively such control and improvement activities are implemented, the higher the level of equipment improvement that can be achieved. Do not try to take the easy way by leaving everything to equipment improvement teams. To achieve effective improvement, the division requesting the session must take the initiative to check in advance, during routine control and improvement activities, whether all the necessary data and tools are present and correct, and rectify matters if they are not.

A further key to the success of an equipment-improvement session is to ensure during the advance preparations that the team leader and the division requesting the improvement are aiming at the same level of improvement and not working at cross-purposes.

Experimentation

In an equipment-improvement session, much time is spent observing actual objects and equipment at the actual scene of the problem. In an atmosphere of urgency, the team members discard all biases, fixed ideas, and "common sense," and give top priority to manipulating the existing situation to see what happens. They start by uncovering problems, then proceed to consider them, evaluate them, then instigate large numbers of improvements as countermeasures. Their basic approach is to test improvement suggestions before debating them theoretically, and thereby avoid jumping to negative conclusions. They take the attitude that it is perfectly acceptable to put an incorrect plan into action if it is quickly modified or changed to another plan.

Even if there is not enough time to fabricate the equipment required by a plan, a makeshift trial can be carried out on the same day — by, for example, using staff to compensate for lack of machinery. Through such measures, the team tries to ensure that the improvement plans are promptly put into practice and that the improvement is completed in a single day.

Decision and Follow-Up

To ensure that the improvement topics bequeathed by the team are followed up by the division, a person must be placed in charge and a time limit specified. At the final presentation meeting, section managers from the division requesting the improvement thank the team members and express their resolve to achieve real results in the follow-up process. A follow-up meeting is held one or two months later to check the results.

An equipment improvement is like a drama that starts with plot preparations, builds to a climax on the actual improvement day, and draws to a conclusion at the follow-up meeting. Besides training team members to analyze quality data, a further aim of equipment improvement is to develop quality engineers capable of preventing defects in advance. This is accomplished by detecting workplace malfunctions and minor flaws that signal the production of defects, assessing them, and taking corrective action.

Examples of Quality Component Maintenance

The following are typical examples of malfunctions and minor defects in quality components (on which MQP management focuses) and the maintenance of such components. These examples are intended to point out the key equipment parts that require attention at Furukawa Electric (see Figure 6-1).

Example 1: Blockages due to copper powder and other foreign matter in coolant. If copper particles or other foreign matter cause obstructions inside the die and its housing in a wire-drawing machine (a machine that draws copper wire through a die), the wire may break or dimensional inaccuracies may occur. To avoid this, dies are constantly washed with coolant and the amounts of copper powder and other foreign matter in the coolant are measured.

Example 2: Blockage of strainers in coolant lines. In water-cooled equipment, in-line strainers can be blocked by contaminants. This impedes water flow, lowers pressure, and affects cooling capacity. Strainers are therefore cleaned periodically and their level of contamination checked. Variation in coolant pressure and temperature is also constantly monitored.

Example 3: Oscillation of guide mechanism. In bobbin winders, winding defects occur if there is play in the guide mechanism or if the wire oscillates relative to the guide rollers. These must be constantly checked.

Example 4: Guide roller wear. Worn guide rollers can scratch the wire, so a continual damage check is required.

Example 5: Surface damage to wire by felt pads. Felt pads are provided to remove foreign matter, but contamination or displacement of these pads can cause surface damage or breakage of the product. The pads are therefore regularly inspected and replaced.

Example 6: Deformation of bobbin spool and scratching of inner face. Winding defects occur if the bobbin spools on which the product is wound are deformed, while scratches on the inner faces of these spools damage the surface of the product. Inspection of items such as bobbin spools is easily overlooked, but it is important.

Example 1: Blockages Due to Copper Powder and Other Foreign Matter in Coolant

die

+   +

filter arrangement   copper powder

wear, scratches

intrusion of foreign object

obstruction

Example 2: Blockage of Strainers in Coolant Lines

Check hydraulic pressure, temperature, level of contamination

Example 3: Oscillation of Guide Mechanism

oscillation

copper wire

guide roller

Example 4: Guide Roller Wear

wear

Example 5: Surface Damage to Wire by Felt Pads

vertical displacement

Example 6: Deformation of Bobbin Spool and Scratching of Inner Face

scratching of inner face   deformation of rim

Example 7: Contamination and Misalignment of Beam Sensors

Example 9: Contamination of Coolant Channels

mold

coolant

Example 8: Wear and Corrosion of Contacts and Looseness of Screws

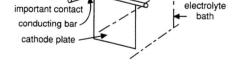

important contact
conducting bar
cathode plate

electrolyte bath

Figure 6-1. Quality Components and Their Abnormalities

Example 10: Wear and Breakage of Dies, Jigs, and Tools

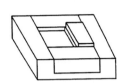

Example 11: Wire Speed Variation

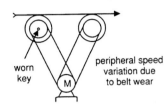

worn key

peripheral speed variation due to belt wear

Example 12: Play in Automatic Chucks

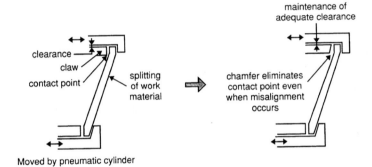

maintenance of adequate clearance

clearance

claw

contact point

splitting of work material

chamfer eliminates contact point even when misalignment occurs

Moved by pneumatic cylinder

Example 13: Tension Variation Due to Spring Elasticity Dispersion and Roller Wear

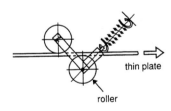

thin plate

roller

Example 14: Need to Check Foreign Matter When Cleaning Filters

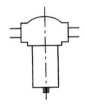

Example 7: Contamination and misalignment of sensor beams. Idling and minor stoppages (when the work is temporarily halted) can be caused by contamination or misalignment of sensor beams.

Example 8: Wear and corrosion of contacts and looseness of screws. If there is wear or corrosion at the point of contact between a cathode plate and the conducting bar in an electrolyte bath, the potential difference or the current can be affected. The same problem can happen if the screws at the base of the conducting bar are loose, so it is essential that these are checked.

Example 9: Contamination of coolant channels. If the channels through which the coolant passes in molds are contaminated by scale, oil, or dirt then cooling capacity will be affected and defects will be produced in the ingots. The level of contamination in the channels is measured during cleaning.

Example 10: Wear and breakage of dies, jigs, or tools. Product defects are caused by loss of accuracy, wear, and breakage of dies, jigs, or tools. Concern yourselves not only with product quality (the result) but also with its cause (i.e., the precision with which dies, jigs, and tools are assembled, and any loss of accuracy or deterioration in these).

Example 11: Wire speed variation. Wire stock must sometimes be kept running at a fixed speed. Variations in speed can be caused by belt slippage or by loosening of a pulley wheel as a result of a worn key securing the pulley to the shaft. Belts and keys must be checked regularly.

Example 12: Play in automatic chucks. Play in an automatic chuck creates a gap and causes the work to be held by the leading edge of the claw, which can cause damage. Maintain adequate clearance and chamfer the edge of the claw so that point contact cannot occur even if the claw is displaced.

Example 13: Variation in spring tension and roller wear. Pairs of rollers used to maintain a thin metal plate under constant tension and remove water from its surface do not function properly if there is variation in spring tension or if there are worn areas on the roller surfaces. Springs and rollers are therefore checked regularly.

Example 14: Accumulation of foreign matter in filters. When cleaning fluid, cutting oil, plating solution, and other liquids contain foreign objects larger than the dimensions permitted, scratches may be caused. Filters located along the flow routes of such liquids are therefore regularly dismantled and foreign matter adhering to the filter elements is removed. The purpose of this is not to clean the elements but to check the amount of foreign matter collected, find out where it is coming from, and eliminate it.

EIGHT STEPS FOR DEPLOYING MQP MANAGEMENT THROUGH EQUIPMENT IMPROVEMENT

This section explains how to put MQP management into practice and describes eight steps for deploying it through equipment improvement. The key points for doing this are explained at each step.

Step 1: Analyze and Verify the Present State of Quality Defect Production

The aim of this step is to analyze and verify the existing situation by answering questions such as "What kind of defects have been produced in what quantities up to now?" and, "In eliminating defects, with which process and which type of defect should we begin?"

First clarify the relationship between the required qualities and the control characteristics. Then proceed by organizing defect phenomena by product, and plotting them on a defects map or defects process matrix to indicate clearly how many defects of each kind are being produced in each process.

Then select defects to be used as improvement topics. Chronic defects are usually selected, but those more easily treated may also be chosen.

Once a topic has been selected, the existing and ideal situations regarding that topic are analyzed and studied until they are understood in depth. Accomplish this by examining actual defects in the workplace if necessary, as well as data such as microphotographs, defect records, work orders, work standards, and autonomous maintenance calendars (which should already be in routine use).

Step 2: Prepare and Analyze an MTBQF Analysis Chart

The aim of this step is to identify trends in the occurrence of defects by using data from defect records over the past several years as control data and compiling it on annual charts (see Figures 6-2 and 6-3).

First, prepare a mean time between quality failure (MTBQF) analysis chart on a single sheet of paper by drawing a diagram of the equipment layout and entering on it the defect data for a particular year in chronological sequence, classified according to cause and phenomenon. Do this in such a way that it is possible to tell at a glance what defects occurred at what intervals as a result of the deterioration of which components, and what losses resulted. How this data is organized into categories is the key to obtaining useful information for subsequent improvement activities. If three of these analysis charts are prepared for three consecutive years, they will instantly show the defects picture over that period of time, and will indicate the frequency of defects that occur regularly over long periods. The required information can be made available at any time by keeping these charts in the workplace and updating them constantly. Displaying them also facilitates discussion of defects countermeasures and MQP management action.

Step 3: Monitor, Survey, and Measure in the Workplace

The aim of this step is to understand the principles, functions, and mechanisms by which processing takes place. This is done by gathering results of the defect data analysis performed in the previous step, and collecting equipment drawings, catalogs, autonomous maintenance materials, production orders, and other materials. This information is used as a basis for closely monitoring the way in which processing actually takes place and the current state of the equipment, using measuring instruments when needed. An increased interest in and understanding of the equipment must be shown when doing this, and explanatory diagrams are prepared as necessary. Factors regarded as possible causes of defects are tracked down by repeatedly asking *Why?* and many problem areas suspected of being conditions for defect production are exposed. When autonomous maintenance is not yet fully established, emphasis is first placed on achieving this goal.

As preparation for this step, promotion of the eight steps for autonomous maintenance and visual control must have been established (see Figure 3-9). In addition, operators must have developed the basic skills required for these activities.

The procedure for this step begins with an understanding of the functions and mechanisms of how defects are created, and pinpointing the relationships between problem areas or malfunctions and defect phenomena. This is accomplished by visiting the workplace to measure and observe the processing conditions and the state of the equipment while quizzing operators on their know-how and past experiences. A major point in eliminating defects is whether good understanding can be obtained and problem areas exposed at this stage. To clarify detailed points, draw diagrams on one-point lesson sheets to aid discussion.

The problems identified are illustrated or described on cards by individual participants, and summarized on a quality

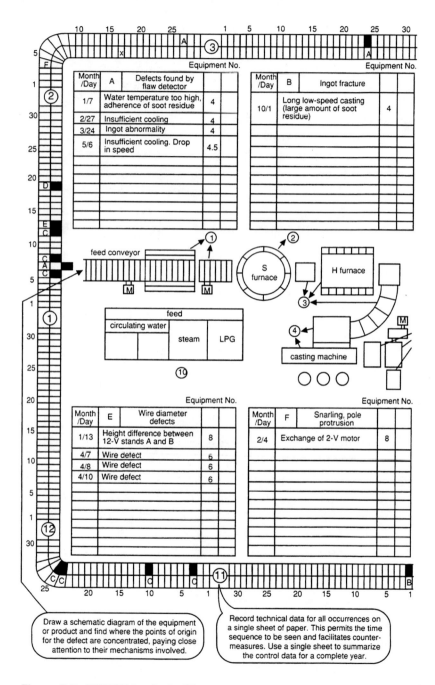

Figure 6-2. MTBQF Analysis Chart

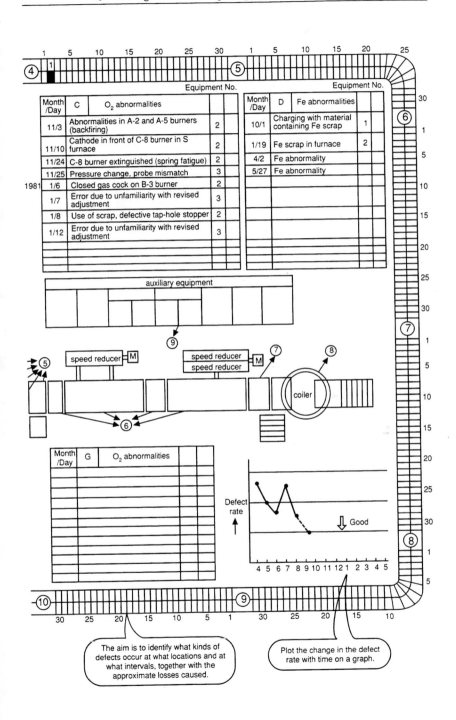

Type of defect							
No..	Month /day	Equipment No.	Condition of work	Type of product	Location	Cause	Amount of loss
1							
2							

Figure 6-3. Example of MTBQF Analysis Form

component map (see Figure 6-4). The MQP analysis and identification chart described in the next step is prepared using the map illustrated in Figure 6-4.

Step 4: Prepare an MQP Analysis and Identification Chart

Once a systematic understanding has been obtained of the relationship between the defect phenomena and the deficiencies in processing and equipment conditions that cause those defects, the data are recorded on an MQP analysis and identification chart to clarify the causes. Preparation of this chart is the aim of this step, and is the main point of this entire chapter. It is an indispensable tool for identifying inaccuracies in processing and equipment conditions and imprecision in human actions.

To proceed, use the individual cards completed in the workplace, and investigate the mechanism that created the defect by persistently asking "Why?" Analyze and enumerate causes of the defect from the way in which the defects manifest themselves. On a MQP analysis and identification chart, record those deficiencies in processing and equipment conditions that constitute causes. Use the final "Why?" to probe down as far as imprecision in human actions.

Next, to prevent defects, clarify the standards required for processing conditions and the accuracy of quality components. Leave a blank space if these are unknown at this stage, and clarify them in the next step (Step 5). At the same time, when an improvement item comes up during the course of discussion, note

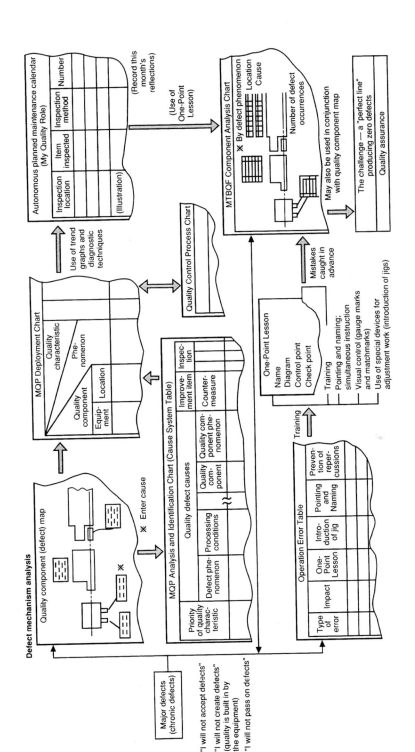

Figure 6-4. Deployment of MQP Management

it in the appropriate space on the identification chart and proceed promptly to implement an improvement plan. Keep the identification chart as simple as possible by omitting anything already recorded on the autonomous maintenance calendar.

Figure 6-5 is an analysis and identification chart for uneven winding of sheet material, while Figure 6-6 is a similar chart for reducing losses arising from surplus wire left over after twisting.

Step 5: Fill in Details on MQP Analysis and Identification Chart

The aim of this step is find the optimum production conditions and search for the ideal settings. This is accomplished by making observations and performing experiments in the workplace on items not recorded on the MQP analysis and identification chart, then gradually filling in the details on the chart. In addition, the aim is to evaluate the existing situation by inspecting and investigating in accordance with the chart, to correct deficiencies, and to move toward work improvement and hardware improvement.

To proceed, stop the equipment and perform observations and experiments based on the key zero defects points listed below. Determine suitable control standards for processing conditions and accuracy tolerances for quality components, and specify inspection methods. Grade the existing control level (A, B, C, or D), and perform maintenance or improvement on items falling short of the mark.

Key Points for Achieving Zero Defects

1. Autonomous maintenance must be properly performed step by step, and operators must be interested in their equipment.
2. The control limits for processing conditions must be clearly set and the conditions must stay within those limits.

Defect Phenomenon	Relevant Process			Defect Mechanism (Primary Cause)	Secondary Cause	Tertiary Cause	Standard (Control of Conditions)	Quality Component	Accuracy of Quality Component	Grade	Improvement Details
Inconsistent winding	O	O	O	Spool deformation	Not inspected	—	To be inspected weekly by work team	Spool	Internal diameter Omm +/-Omm External diameter Omm +/-Omm	D	Measure
				Worn cutter knife	Knives sharpened according to standards but some worn beyond limit	—	Check amount of wear before sharpening (using limit sample)	Cutter knife	Limit sample for amount of wear	D	Check each knife and take action on any worn beyond the limit
				Spacer ring	—	—		Spacer ring	Burrs and soiling Width Omm +/-Omm	D	Measure
				Clearance and overlap	Adjustment with dial gauge and thickness gage		One-Point Lesson			A B	
				Restraining plate			One-Point Lesson			C	
				S-shaped roller	Levelness and parallelism Wear		Measure and set	Roller	Wear External diameter Omm +/-Omm Circularity		Repair upper roller Request engineering department to measure
				Restraining roller	Levelness and parallelism Wear		Measure and set	Roller	Wear External diameter Omm +/-Omm Circularity		Repair upper roller Request engineering department to measure
				Take-up reel	Levelness and parallelism Wear		Measure and set	Roller	Wear External diameter Omm +/-Omm Circularity		Repair upper roller Request engineering department to measure position by attaching gauge to innermost end
				Speed variation of drive roller			Measure	Control device	—		"
				Display fluctuation			Measure	Control device	—		"
				Separator							Request engineering department to install new separator near winding shaft

Figure 6-5. MQP Analysis and Identification Chart

Defect Phenomenon	Relevant Process — Wire drawing	Relevant Process — Wire twisting	Defect Mechanism (Primary Cause)	Secondary Cause	Tertiary Cause	Standard (Control of Conditions)	Quality component	Accuracy of quality component	Grade	Improvement Details
Variation in surplus wire after twisting (too much left over)	O		Capstan slippage (tension variation)	Difference in tension between left- and right-hand spools (30 m)	Different conditions needed on left and right	Different standard settings for left and right Subtract OOm.			C	Use dual counters
				Play in capstan	Accuracy control	Control play in gears	Gear backlash	Within 5 mm (use trend graph)	D	
				Drawing-oil temperature	Temperature variation	30 ~ 50 °C			C	
				Drawing-oil viscosity	Viscosity variation	OO ~ OO -P			C	
				Splitting	Variation in die diameter	Separate supervision of dies	Dies	Internal diameter +/- 1/100 mm	B	
			Counter error	Wrong setting Counter failure		Educate through One-Point Lessons	Counter		C / C	
		O	Variation in bobbin braking during wire twisting	Variation during checking (zero adjustment preferable)		Record and track down causes			B	
				Reproducibility when loosening and tightening		As above			B	
			Control of surplus	Accuracy of brake itself			Brake linings and springs	O O O / O O O	C / C	Install brake conformance tester
				Record amount of surplus for each lot and track down causes	Identify relationship between amount of surplus and braking force	Record data and track down causes (record maximum, minimum, and average surpluses)			C	
		O	Brake body				Brake temperature	OO ~ OO °C	D	Heat or cool

Figure 6-6. MQP Analysis and Identification Chart

3. Quality components and their accuracy tolerances must be clearly identified and must fall within the control limits not just when starting operation but at the end (before servicing) as well. Far too often, no attention is given to the state of equipment after use even though certain parts are bound to deteriorate or become dirty.
4. All adjustment work must be identified and efforts made to eliminate it.
5. Actual equipment, tools, and other objects must be closely observed from various angles using all five senses, especially touch. Many causes of defects are easily overlooked.
6. Pay particular attention to accuracy in factors such as play, eccentricity, and temperature variation.
7. Equipment functions and mechanisms must be understood.

Putting Improvement Proposals into Practice

Improvement proposals may be classified as A (to be implemented immediately), B (within two weeks), C (within approximately one month), or D (to be stored in an idea bank). A person is appointed to take charge of each improvement, with those in group A being tackled immediately.

Step 6: Prepare an MQP Deployment Chart

The aim of this step is to pick from the MQP analysis and identification chart those processing conditions and quality components that must be controlled. The purpose is to determine factors such as failure mode, inspection methods and standards, quality impact, number, control classification, inspection frequency, person responsible and action required, and to summarize these on an MQP deployment chart (see Figure 6-7). When doing this, record on the chart the plans for the regular activities, education, and training needed to eliminate human errors, along with the frequency with which they are to take place.

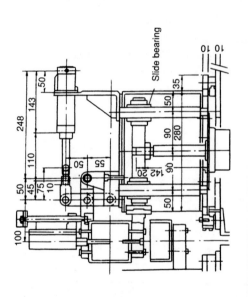

Slide bearing

No.	Item	Phenomenon	Method	Standard	Quality Impact	Number	Control Classification	Frequency	Division Responsible	Action
1	Bolts, nuts, and screws	Looseness	Tighten	Within 90°	Idling and minor stoppages	8 per team		Monthly	Manufacturing	Red matchmarks Locking devices
2	"	"	Match-marks	"	"	"		Monthly	"	"

No.	Item	Check item	Method	Standard				Frequency		Remarks
3	Pneumatic cylinders for swings	Speedometer slackness	Tighten	No slackness	"				"	
4	"	Horizontal play	Move by hand	Within ○○mm	"	10	Trend graph	Monthly	"	
5	"	Vertical play	"	Within ○○mm	"	10	"	"	"	
6	Die nozzle diameter	Wear	Magnifying glass	8 + 0.6 mm − 0	"	10		Whenever used	"	Record history of each die
7	Tapered face of die	Smooth for approx. 8 mm	Visual inspection	—	"	"		"	"	Remove residues with spatula
8	Nozzle tip diameter	Wear	Magnifying glass	Suitable for die nozzle diameter	"	"		"	"	
9	End face of nozzle	Unevenness	"	Should be smooth	"	"		"	"	
10	Spatula	Wear	"	4-mm radius	"			"	"	
11	Air pressure	Variation	Gauge mark	4± 0.5 kg/cm²	"			Daily		
12	Air 3-point set	Zero oil consumption	Supply oil	Drops from upper mark to lower mark				Monthly		
13	"	Sump full	Drain sump					Daily		

Figure 6-7. MQP Deployment Chart for Zero Adjustment

Make the MQP deployment chart as concrete as possible. To do so, provide a schematic diagram or other drawing at the top of the chart illustrating the parts to be inspected and recording the inspection procedure and standard inspection times. This makes the chart easier to understand and facilitates efficient inspection. When defects originate more from human actions than from the equipment, identify and record the mistakes on an MQP deployment chart, then move toward preventing them from happening again by introducing devices such as gauges or by providing the necessary training (pointing and naming) (see Figure 6-8).

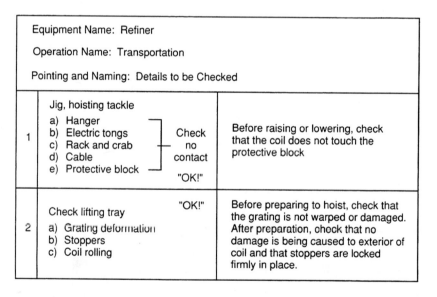

Figure 6-8. Quality Pointing and Naming

Step 7: Review Maintenance Calendar and Provide Education

The aim of this step is to prepare calendars for autonomous quality maintenance and planned quality maintenance, as well as to provide education using one-point lessons and other methods. The handling and inspection tasks shown on the MQP analysis, identification, and deployment charts must be standardized, and these standards must be understood and practiced by every worker.

Staff cannot simply explain then hand over freshly prepared deployment charts and maintenance calendars to workers because the charts will not be understood well enough to allow the workers to follow what has been decided. Proper inspection depends greatly on the reliability of individual workers, so it is important that the division and section managers allow them the necessary time to perform the inspections, and train them in the required skills.

Create a situation in which individual workers voluntarily set up their own quality action plans under titles such as "My Quality Role." By preparing maintenance calendars and one-point lessons and by teaching each other and understanding through repetition, workers will become accustomed to following the set procedures correctly.

Use visual controls used widely in the workplace by sign-posting inspection locations, using gauge marks, and so on (see Figure 6-9). This enables anyone to perform inspections and eliminates discrepancies between individuals.

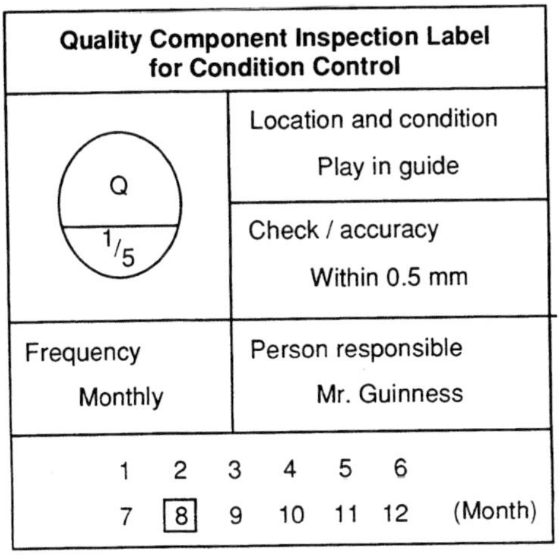

Quality Component Inspection Label for Condition Control	
Q 1/5	Location and condition Play in guide
	Check / accuracy Within 0.5 mm
Frequency Monthly	Person responsible Mr. Guinness
1 2 3 4 5 6 7 [8] 9 10 11 12 (Month)	

Figure 6-9. Quality Component Inspection Label

Also, ensure that everyone readily understands the tolerance limits for the accuracy of quality components and products. To do so, provide samples of these components and products that are beyond tolerance limits, and display them near the equipment. Label each sample for quick reference to its condition.

Step 8: Confirm Results

When the measures described in Steps 1 through 7 have been taken, check the results. If the target has not been reached, repeat the steps from the beginning after suitable reflection. Even if the objective was reached, review the improvement and record the significant points in the form of a case study.

INVESTIGATING SPECIFIC TECHNOLOGY — A PRECONDITION FOR ZERO DEFECTS

In MQP management, investigating and mastering specific equipment technology makes an indispensable basis for taking action against defects.

If there are any points not understood or problems that cannot be solved, the assistance of third parties is actively sought. When doing this, it is important not to leave everything to such people but to try to understand the problem by having it explained with the aid of drawings and illustrations. Engineers are often experts in their own fields but surprisingly ignorant about minor points of specific technology in other fields. Difficult problems can often be solved by listening carefully to outside parties and making use of their expertise. The following example illustrates this point:

In heating equipment, actions taken against defects are aided by making full use of specific thermal control techniques (for both heating and cooling). Thermal control is not only important as an integral part of any energy-saving program; the wasteful consumption of energy in the repeated heating and cooling of this equipment often causes variations in temperature and other processing conditions that adversely affect product quality (see Figure 6-10).

Because of this, it is important to keep constant track of thermal efficiencies and the amounts of energy used in producing a product unit as well as understanding energy consumption mechanisms.

MQP management consists of applying the ideas and procedures of preventive maintenance to the challenge of achieving zero quality defects by identifying all conceivable relevant factors and taking action against them before they become problems.

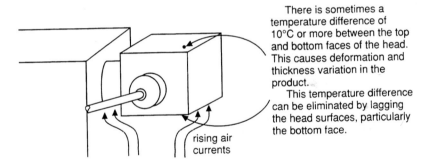

There is sometimes a temperature difference of 10°C or more between the top and bottom faces of the head. This causes deformation and thickness variation in the product.

This temperature difference can be eliminated by lagging the head surfaces, particularly the bottom face.

rising air currents

Figure 6-10. Plastic Extruder

7

Planned Quality Maintenance

This chapter describes the deployment of planned quality maintenance spearheaded by maintenance personnel as required by Step 7 of Chapter 6.

DEPLOYING PLANNED MAINTENANCE

Planned maintenance is led by maintenance personnel but with operator participation. It consists of regular intensive servicing carried out periodically with the equipment stopped. It could also be regarded as ongoing equipment improvement aimed at eliminating failures and defects.

Autonomous maintenance is deployed with operators in the leading role. Planned maintenance, on the other hand, is the basic activity performed by maintenance specialists. The benefits that any division derives from its maintenance activities depends largely on the level of planned maintenance, which varies considerably.

The Aims of Planned Maintenance

1. To correct minor flaws and abnormalities (restore equipment to the ideal state and service areas that cannot be reached during daily maintenance)
2. To perform periodic measurement and diagnosis (control accuracy)
3. To exchange parts periodically (replace parts that show wear or that deteriorate through friction or contact)
4. To disassemble, inspect, and overhaul periodically (rotating machinery, gearboxes, and so on)
5. To implement improvements (increase access to hard-to-inspect places, prolong equipment life, etc.)
6. To educate (train operators on set topics, encourage self-study by maintenance personnel, etc.)
7. To perform inspection and improvement from MQP analysis and identification charts

Planned maintenance determines the most appropriate times to deal with minor flaws and abnormalities discovered while the equipment is running, carry out regular disassembly and overhauls, and various improvements. These activities are undertaken chiefly by maintenance personnel but with operators also participating. Planned maintenance consists of concrete action incorporating planned education which allows all participants to rotate the PDCA cycle and gain a great sense of satisfaction.

Planned quality maintenance is the term used to describe maintenance that focuses not only on the types of failures that halt equipment, but also on those that reduce quality and cause functional deterioration. It is performed on quality components enumerated during MQP management. Planned quality maintenance is promoted as one of the main pillars of a defect-prevention program, and yields significant benefits.

Promoting Planned Maintenance

In planned maintenance, priority is given to the more important equipment. Major equipment items are ranked in three classes (A, B, and C) depending on factors such as the existing level of control, degree of reliability required, and operation rate (see Figure 7-1).

Prepare an annual calendar. Perform planned maintenance in accordance with an annual calendar prepared on the basis of inspection standards, analysis of past data, information from drawings, workplace observations, and so on. Reduce the planned maintenance load by keeping in mind the following guidelines related to inspection items:

- As much as possible, try to convert periodic inspection items to daily inspection or patrol inspection items. Do so by improving access to places that are difficult to inspect.
- Use diagnostic techniques to troubleshoot during maintenance patrols, employing the condition-based maintenance approach.
- Treat small maintenance jobs taking less than 30 minutes as *unplanned maintenance.*

Try to review maintenance periods and inspection methods every time planned maintenance is performed.

Carry out advance preparation. The beneficial effects of planned maintenance are multiplied by preparation and planning. List the jobs to be performed, and give any necessary training at least one week in advance (see Figure 7-2). This allows you to prepare for the number of work-hours needed, and to ensure that the required parts and tools are boxed and left in a designated place for prompt issue on the day they are required for the maintenance work.

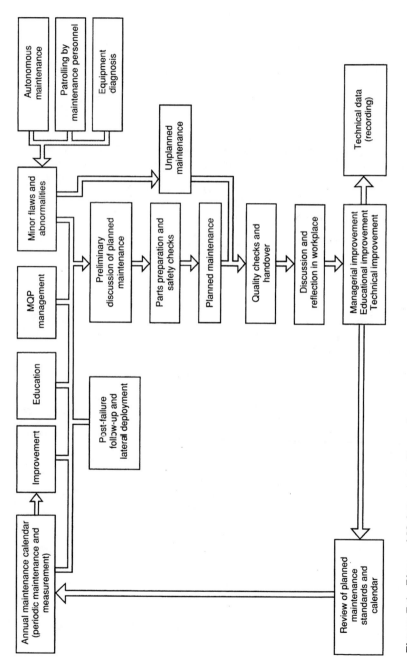

Figure 7-1. Planned Maintenance Procedure

Equipment Name	—	Section Manager	Staff Member	Team Leader
Scheduled Date	7/25			

No.	Location	Item	Work-hours Required (No. of Persons × h)	Person in charge	Parts	Checks Safety	Checks Quality	Countermeasures, impressions, etc.
1	Control panels	Tightening	1 × 1	Dickinson	—	Display "Under Inspection" sign	—	Recheck loose screws (red marks)
2	"	Replace contact parts (relays and switches)	1 × 2	Dickinson	Relays and switches	"	—	Display replacement dates. No attention was being paid to lifetimes.
3	Rotating machinery	Wash and varnish coils	2 × 5	Donovan Fields	Varnish	—	—	
4	"	Replace brushes	1 × 3	Dickinson	Brushes	—	—	Education was lacking

Reflections, observations, good impressions, etc.:

More study needed of the skills required for disassembling and maintaining rotating machinery.

Figure 7-2. Planned Maintenance Items for July

Coordinate schedule with production control division. If there is no set time each day during which production stops, it is necessary to arrange with the production control division the specific days and times each month when the equipment will be stopped for planned maintenance.

During busy periods, planned maintenance often must be scheduled for holidays, and a system devised beforehand to cope with the busy periods. In order to avoid disrupting subsequent processes when equipment is stopped for planned maintenance, complete in advance the amount of work corresponding to the amount that would normally be produced during the planned downtime.

Carry out planned maintenance. The operator always takes part when planned maintenance is performed on a piece of equipment, and maintenance personnel pass on their skills by giving practical guidance. Assure safety when doing this by performing safety checks in accordance with *accident-prevention training* or other safety programs. Parts that have deteriorated and need replacing are excellent information sources and teaching tools. The basis of productive maintenance is establishing clear standards for parts replacement as well as measuring, observing, and recording the accuracy and degree of deterioration of parts when they are replaced.

Planned maintenance follow-up. After a planned maintenance job has been completed, those concerned always have a short discussion and reflection to marshal the results. They analyze the experience, the knowledge acquired from abnormalities and problems they discovered, the topics left to tackle, the inspection methods they used, and any points requiring further study. This information is put in order and reflected in the next round of activities. The planned maintenance execution rate (the ratio between the number of maintenance jobs planned and those actually completed) is calculated and controlled (see Figure 7-3).

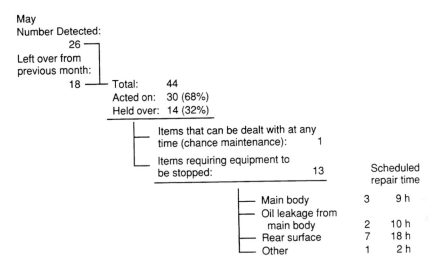

Figure 7-3. Numbers of Minor Flaws Detected During Daily Maintenance; Planned Maintenance Execution Rate

Planned maintenance guarantees. If a machine breaks down despite having undergone planned maintenance, painstakingly investigate why the failure occurred and why you were unable to detect it at the time. Once a planned maintenance job has been completed, the performance of the equipment should be guaranteed for at least a month, until the next planned service takes place. Sometimes planned maintenance has the opposite of the intended effect, with the number of failures increasing and the equipment condition worsening. Efforts should be made to reduce the number of times maintenance staff are recalled to deal with such problems.

Measuring Deterioration

Particular emphasis has been placed in recent years on measuring deterioration, and this is performed during both planned maintenance and patrol maintenance (with the equipment running). Use diagnostic equipment available commercially or developed in-house to measure signs of deterioration and detect minor flaws and abnormalities before failures occur. However, even though this equipment may be used, nothing is as reliable or important as the five senses, and these activities should be based on human judgment. Answers to questions such as, "What is the current state of the equipment?", "Can it be used in this condition?", "Should it be stopped and repaired right away?", and "How will this affect product quality?" must always be based on human assessments. Personal judgment is vital in deciding whether immediate action is required.

From Time-based Maintenance (TBM) to Condition-based Maintenance (CBM)

As a result of the development and use of diagnostic techniques and equipment, more and more measurement activities can be incorporated into planned maintenance. The aim, of course, is more efficient prevention of failures and defects with fewer work-hours. Time-based maintenance, in which parts considered likely to deteriorate are replaced at fixed intervals, generally increases maintenance costs and often actually impairs reliability. Concentrate, therefore, on condition-based maintenance, in which abnormalities are predicted through measurements using diagnostic equipment. However, from the viewpoint of overall cost, it is often more economical to replace small, frequent-failure items before they fail than to monitor their condition.

Diagnostic methods

There are two diagnostic methods:

- Methods in which equipment condition is measured at a particular point in time and abnormalities are detected using that information alone.

- Methods in which data is collected at regular intervals starting with equipment in its normal condition, and abnormalities are detected from the trend of the data with time.

Diagnostic instruments include stethoscopes; vibration and sound level indicators; thermometers; thickness gauges; oil samplers and analyzers; oil filters; insulation testers; stroboscopes; pressure gauges; ammeters and voltmeters; flow detectors; magnifying glasses; spirit levels; endoscopes; feeler gauges; relay testers; ohmmeters; synchroscopes; infrared imagers; and dial gauges.

The most important thing from now on will be to master new unsystematized diagnostic techniques. The key point is the extent to which diagnostic and inspection methods can be developed that can be used while equipment is running. As progress is made in this area, equipment operating rates will improve and reliability will be enhanced.

Unplanned Maintenance

Sometimes abnormalities detected during autonomous maintenance or other activities require small, urgent repairs which cannot wait until the next planned maintenance or servicing day. Minor overhauls may also need to be completed in a short time. Perform such jobs when equipment is stopped briefly for changeover or is idle for various reasons such as during mealtimes, or during a major breakdown.

In performing these jobs, place maintenance job cards on dispatch boards and individual weekly schedule boards. These cards should clearly show the job titles and schedules for each piece of equipment so anyone can understand them at a glance. This enables the maintenance crew to mobilize as soon as the production control division contacts them.

Everybody's heart sinks when a machine breaks down, but at the same time people need to see equipment stoppages as opportunities to perform maintenance. This kind of chance maintenance further lightens the planned maintenance load.

Attitudes of Maintenance Personnel

To build an effective planned maintenance system, maintenance personnel must be at a higher level of readiness and perform more advanced work than operators in the area of productive maintenance.

Maintenance personnel must be determined, through *prediction* and *prevention*, never to permit failures or defects to occur. They must realize that their true task is not carrying out repairs but eliminating failures. If they cannot answer when asked for their equipment operating rate or quality defect rate, it proves they lack the right awareness and are not qualified to undertake predictive and preventive activities. In the past, maintenance personnel often looked smug the next morning when thanked for showing up in the middle of the night to fix a breakdown that the night-shift operators could not handle. This is absurd; maintenance staff should not have to be reminded that their basic mission is to ensure that breakdowns do not occur at any time, night or day.

Maintenance personnel should decide which items of equipment they are responsible for and do their utmost to prevent failures in that equipment. Clearly specify each person's maintenance role on individual weekly schedules and monthly action plans. This enables preventive action to be carried out systematically and efficiently in preparation for busy periods.

Maintenance personnel should always try to repair failures swiftly. They should give importance to preparation and training, promptly discovering causes whenever a failure occurs, then making the repairs and checking the equipment before handing it over. They should never simply repair equipment without tracing the causes of failure.

Maintenance personnel must be aware that they are teachers and leaders in the maintenance field. They must learn how to talk convincingly to operators and teach them about autonomous maintenance methods at every opportunity. They must be concerned about reducing materials losses, shortening setup times, eliminating idling and minor stoppages, saving energy, and controlling measurements. They should act in close cooperation with the production division.

In the past, there were problems regarding the definition of a *failure*; people tended to concentrate exclusively on problems that actually brought machinery to a halt. However, if the frequency of this type of failure is reduced, the maintenance division must use its surplus time to cooperate in solving the types of problems just described. Quality, quantity, and cost in the workplace are becoming more and more dependent on the condition of equipment. Maintenance personnel must be fully conversant with not only the stoppage rates for important equipment but also the monthly defect rates and operating rates and how these are determined. They must take action against the types of failures that affect quality and cause deterioration.

Through the following actions, maintenance personnel must create a maintenance workplace trusted by the people on the shop floor:

- Make prompt response and action a habit (by holding machine-side meetings, for example, and setting clear dates for completion of maintenance work).
- Organize and display request slips and equipment chits for each item of equipment.
- Spend time with operators, answer their questions, and give them advice (especially during maintenance patrols).

IMPROVING REPAIR AND MAINTENANCE EFFICIENCY

This section describes methods for reversing equipment deterioration by increasing the efficiency of repair and maintenance activities.

Shortening Repair and Maintenance Times

Repair and maintenance work must be high in quality and swiftly completed. To accomplish this, keep the following points in mind:

- Select and organize tools, maintenance cards, spare parts, and other routine items.
- Teach operators the names of parts to facilitate communication of failure information.
- Supervise and control spare parts.
- Prepare a board showing the location of maintenance personnel at any time.
- Devise measures for dealing with locations that are difficult to inspect and hard to repair.
- Take action against the causes of failures.
- Clarify work procedures.
- Clarify procedures for identifying causes.
- Replace whole units rather than individual parts where possible ("changeineering").
- Investigate recycling techniques.
- Perform safety checks when starting work and quality checks on completion.
- Extend equipment life by raising maintenance quality, and try to eliminate repeat call-outs.
- Whenever a failure of intermediate or higher severity has occurred, discuss methods and procedures for repairing it in about half the previously required time. This will help to reduce the time required to deal with subsequent failures.

Preventing Failure Recurrence

Maintenance personnel must realize that remedial action to deal with failures is completely different from measures taken to prevent failures from recurring. When a failure occurs, it must be fixed, and remedial action must always be taken. However, complete prevention of recurrence cannot be assured if managers and supervisors do not follow up carefully enough. When a failure occurs, first trace its cause. Some possible causes of failure are shown in Figure 7-4.

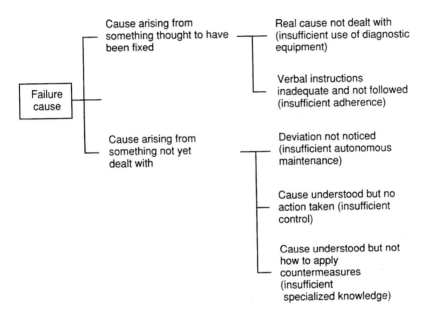

Figure 7-4. Types of Failure Causes

By repeating the question *Why?* at least three times, you probe the situation to find out why the problem was not detected beforehand and why the failure was not anticipated. Continue this until you have narrowed the cause to human action, and then eliminate it. Only when this kind of advance action is properly planned and firmly established does it become recurrence prevention.

Preventing failures from recurring, however, is easier to say than to do. The difficulty lies in making sure that the obvious is done thoroughly. Vigilance is often relaxed and similar failures are allowed to occur soon after improvement activities, with the result that the overall number of failures does not decrease. To avoid this, prevention must be inculcated as the basic mindset and method of action. Only then will the number of failures decline. Hardware improvements are often given priority in recurrence prevention, and this may sometimes be effective; however, failures do not generally decrease with this approach. You must first institute managerial improvements, then, if these prove insufficient, proceed with hardware improvements. Managerial improvement with its sights unwaveringly set on the ultimate goal of *prevention* will make the basic strategy one of attacking the true causes of failures.

Upgrading Servicing and Recycling Technology

With the aim of speeding and improving the quality of servicing, provide maintenance personnel with as many surface tables, machine tools, and other maintenance equipment as possible. This will enable them to repair small recyclable parts, and to repair cracked parts themselves by techniques such as thermal spraying or fillet welding.

Maintenance Quality

Since poor quality maintenance work leads to mistakes that can immediately produce failures and defects, maintenance quality is a topic that cannot be ignored. Disassembled parts must not be placed directly on the floor or other dirty surface, and must be arranged in sequence to facilitate reassembly. This is only one of many such points that must be considered. Another example: Bearing lubricants must be changed in a clean area to prevent contamination.

Critical Defect Component Analysis

Ordinary breakdowns and defects can be eliminated by the thorough application of autonomous maintenance and planned maintenance. However, critical failure component analysis is needed to deal with failures and defects which rarely happen but which have a very severe impact when they do. These must be avoided at all costs. The approach is to imagine the effect of a particular failure. Then envision how it could be dealt with, investigate predictive methods using diagnostic technology and various types of sensors, find ways to prolong the life of parts, and ensure that spare parts are readily available.

ELIMINATING IDLING AND MINOR STOPPAGES

Idling and minor stoppages refers to the occasions when machinery stops or runs empty as a result of minor problems. It frequently occurs with automatic processing, assembly, packaging and transfer machinery of relatively high performance and speed. When equipment drawings and instructions are not well understood and the equipment is not monitored closely, it is difficult to find the causes of idling and minor stoppages. It has, therefore, become important to constantly watch, understand and make improvements.

Causes of Idling and Minor Stoppages

There are several categories of idling and minor stoppages (see Figure 7-5):

- Those that are easily dealt with but against which fundamental countermeasures are difficult to take.
- Those caused by abnormalities in the shape of the workpiece as a result of the type of part used or the nature of the previous operation.
- Those due to operating errors.
- Those due to deficiencies in equipment design. For example, consider the following two types of idling and minor stoppage caused by slackness in bolts or screws:

- Those that can be fixed easily by promptly retightening loose bolts or screws
- Those that cannot be fixed without readjustment, because things slip out of line when these bolts and screws become loose

Seven Steps for Eliminating Idling and Minor Stoppages

In attempting to eliminate idling and minor stoppages, it is necessary to expose and deal with minor flaws and malfunctions. It is also necessary to maintain optimal conditions for dimensional accuracy of shapes, restore deteriorated parts, and eliminate the need for adjustment. The following seven steps correspond to the seven steps described earlier for implementation of MQP management.

Collect data using MTBF analysis charts, etc. First, find out the number of times idling and minor stoppages occur. Investigate the number and frequency of occurrences for each problem area and type of incident.

Perform autonomous maintenance and tightening. Ensure that autonomous maintenance is being properly carried out, including cleaning, exposing malfunctions, lubricating, and tightening.

Observe what is happening. Accurate observation at the workplace of what is happening in idling and minor stoppages is fundamental. When the phenomena cannot be understood by visual means alone, check using VTRs, high-speed cameras, etc. Classify the stoppages by their mode of occurrence and infer their causes.

Analyze and understand the mechanisms behind idling and minor stoppages. By repeatedly asking *Why?* clarify the conditions under which idling and minor stoppages occur and record these on the MQP analysis and identification chart previously

System	Type of Phenomenon	Number	Type of Cause	Countermeasure
Transfer	1. Work caught	11	Dimensional inaccuracies (of guides or connector caps), malfunctions, play in parts, clearances	Eliminate adjustment for centering, etc.
	2. Work bent or otherwise deformed	7	Off-center dies and molds, unbalanced temperature distributions	Improve accuracy
	3. Work blocked or jammed	—	Inclusion of foreign matter or different type parts, insufficient pneumatic or hydraulic pressure (insufficient actuation), blocked nozzles, inadequate vacuum pressure	Top up and inspect
	4. Parts run out or oversupplied	—	—	Provide advance warning signals
	5. Misalignment (starting over)		Defective jigs or tools, insufficient training	Maintenance calendar, training
	6. External defects on work	4	Dirt, foreign matter, wear, burrs, adhesion to mold	Action against cause
	7. Work out of position	—	Diagonal gripping by chuck	Modify guide
Assembly (Processing)	8. Malfunction	6	Insufficient air pressure, damaged parts	Give importance to pressure gauges
	9. Misfeed	4	Springs detached, parts fallen off, nuts out of position, gradient incorrect, surface defects	Inspect quality components, perform comprehensive tightness checks
	10. Faulty chucking	2		"
	11. Faulty timing	2		"
	12. Insufficient clearance	—	Burrs, adhesion to mold, scale, chips on chute	Send to chute using compressed air
Inspection	13. Misoperation	10	Displacement, slack, misalignment (e.g., of limit switches, beam sensors, dials, level controls, valves, or electrodes)	Tighten (to cautionary marks), double up, or reposition sensors
	14. Out of position	2	Failure to actuate	

Figure 7-5. Some Causes of Idling and Minor Stoppages and Their Countermeasures

described (see Figures 6-5 and 6-6). Select as causes all situations that could possibly develop with equipment parts under those conditions.

Deal with problems such as eliminating adjustment work. Repeat observations and measurements in the workplace on all those conditions and equipment parts identified in the previous step and compare with the ideal situation. Observe whether any adjustment work is needed, if abnormalities are occurring, and if the required accuracy is being maintained. Deal with deficiencies promptly.

Investigate the optimal conditions. Reconsider the processing conditions and attachment conditions of parts and set the optimal ones.

Maintain conditions using the maintenance calendar. Prepare a maintenance calendar and perform regular daily inspections to maintain the conditions.

ZERO ADJUSTMENT, RIGHT-FIRST-TIME, AND ACCURACY CONTROL

Because adjustment work depends greatly on the experience and skill of the operator, it very easily becomes a source of defects and losses. In the past, adjustment work was considered unavoidable and was rarely subjected to improvement activity. There was a dependance on the experience and skills of veteran workers. Now, however, improvement efforts must focus on eliminating start-up adjustments and getting things right the first time without trial processing (see Figure 7-6).

Various techniques and examples for achieving zero adjustment are listed in Figures 7-7 and 7-8. Technical investigations of this sort produce excellent results not only from the quality aspect but also in reducing costs.

Controlling equipment accuracy is indispensable for eliminating defects that originate with hardware. Measurements of

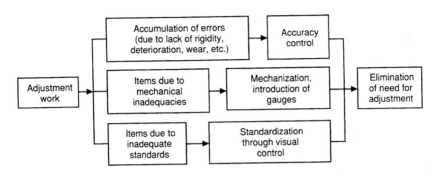

Figure 7-6. Mechanism for Eliminating Adjustment Work

the accuracy of parts that affect quality should be recorded on trend graphs and should always remain within the standards even before the equipment is serviced. The accuracy of measuring instruments must also be controlled. For example, during regular inspections using standard instruments such as pressure gauges, you can provide two outlets so that two gauges can be compared. These could be monitored even during equipment operation.

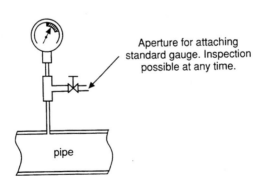

Aperture for attaching standard gauge. Inspection possible at any time.

The results of routine inspection using test pieces depend on the skills of the inspector in the correct handling of instruments and the correct use of measurement methods. These should be checked using QC process charts.

No.	Type of Technique	Specific Case	Specific Action
1	Positioning	Stacking materials, installing dies, mounting guides and frames	Install positioning guides, stops, limit switches, beam sensors, gauges, etc.
2	Centering	Centering nipples, dies, and guides, regulation of traversing, centering of form rollers and nozzles	Use fixed dies
3	Reversing, installing, and removing	Clamps and chucks	Use rotating stands
4	Temperature regulation	—	Preheat
5	Regulation of tension and pressure	Brake application and spring-return tension	Introduce gauges, replace springs as complete sets
6	Regulation of quantities	Mixng of materials, throttling valves, dimension, and dial regulation	Introduce gauges
7	Adjustments necessitated by dimensional inaccuracies	Wear and deterioration	Control accuracy by use of thickness gauges, spacers, and trend graphs
8	Washing	Molds, dies, nipples, tank interiors, rounders	Improve so dirt does not collect, introduce *one-touch washing*
9	Straightening	Slippage or falling-off of work, malfunctioning, blockages, clearing out, starting over, detachment	Introduce chamfers, straightening rollers, etc.
10	Sealing	Dust scattering	Provide air outlets

Figure 7-7. Techniques for Achieving Zero Adjustment

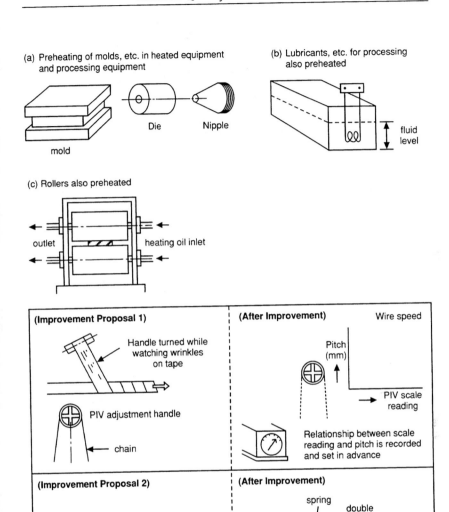

(a) Preheating of molds, etc. in heated equipment and processing equipment

mold

Die   Nipple

(b) Lubricants, etc. for processing also preheated

fluid level

(c) Rollers also preheated

outlet   heating oil inlet

(Improvement Proposal 1)

Handle turned while watching wrinkles on tape

PIV adjustment handle

chain

(After Improvement)   Wire speed

Pitch (mm)

PIV scale reading

Relationship between scale reading and pitch is recorded and set in advance

(Improvement Proposal 2)

Tension measured by spring balance and adjustment performed each time

(After Improvement)

spring   double nut

A single assembly consisting of a spring, threaded shaft and double nut is used. Replaced for different sizes.

Figure 7-8. Achieving Zero Adjustment — Case Study 1 ·
Quality Instability Eliminated by Preheating at Startup

CREATING RELIABLE EQUIPMENT

The important task for manufacturing firms is responding to factory automation and the introduction of flexible manufacturing systems by developing and fabricating extremely reliable equipment which is a pleasure to operate. A company's success or failure in this has become the key to whether it can distinguish itself from its competitors. Developing this equipment requires the collection and use of improvement case studies (see Figure 7-9); the participation of both maintenance and production personnel; and the performance of more equipment improvement and subcontract work in-house.

Improvement case studies and knowledge obtained through MQP management activities on existing processes can be used as educational materials for regular improvement. They should also be turned into a valuable resource for assisting in new equipment designs that increase reliability and maintainability.

People from both the production and maintenance departments should be allowed to participate in equipment development from the design stage. They should help in deciding the design aims and determining what points to consider and what techniques to use in creating equipment that will be a pleasure to operate.

If improvement areas are set up within each workplace and efforts made to develop as many people as possible able to effect improvements, workers will become capable of doing their own improvements and will create outstandingly reliable equipment.

Repair shops can also use their ingenuity and ideas to make equipment without contracting it out. Some examples of improvement ideas include illuminated signboards; transferring equipment with conveyor belts; cleaning equipment stands; data box files; workbenches; safety covers designed for easy inspection; modifications to lubricant piping; receptacles for dies; toolboards; display boxes for limit samples; boards displaying control graphs; and fabrication and installation of various sensors.

Improvement (Proposed/Completed)		Date: _____
		Section: _____
Title		
Before improvement	After improvement	
Points to note		
Benefits	Comments by related parties	Comments by supervisor

Figure 7-9. Improvement Record

MAINTENANCE SKILLS EDUCATION

Maintenance people's skills are important, not simply their numbers. Programs are needed for developing the type of maintenance personnel who will strive to improve their skills and quickly detect and diagnose signs of failure, assess them, and carry out high-quality repairs.

To analyze equipment failures and product losses and track down their causes, maintenance personnel must become well-informed about equipment functions and mechanisms. As much use as possible should be made of drawings, written explanations, catalogs, and specifications. To aid understanding of equipment construction and functions, various kinds of schematic diagrams and maps should also be drawn.

Additional aids to understanding equipment are a knowledge of energy consumption mechanisms and MTBQF analysis.

Maintenance technology must be upgraded in response to advances in equipment. In the past, for example, the designers of computer equipment were often relied on for its maintenance. However, this cannot go on for ever.

Part of the curriculum of an electrical maintenance skills course is shown in Figure 7-10.

Practical Training Curriculum

	AM	PM
Monday	(Travel)	1. Orientation • Introduction to product • Overall outline (control methods, adjustment, maintenance, etc.)
Tuesday	2. Pre-operation checks • Methods for determining polarity of DC motors and turbine generators • Operating sequence • Control power supplies, check pin voltages	3. Waveform observation during operation • Explanation of check pins • Waveforms during normal operation • Oscilloscope practice
Wednesday	4. Adjustment methods • Explanation of adjustment volumes • Speed feedback and current limit settings • Automatic field magnet unit settings	4. Adjustment methods (continued) • Optimum setting of control response • Scale high coder practice
Thursday	5. Auxiliary functions (optional) • HLR, D/A , F/V, printed-circuit boards, etc.	6. Troubleshooting • Fault detection • Discrimination methods for different malfunctions • Daily inspection, data recording
Friday	6. Troubleshooting (continued) • Practical skills (on intentionally created problems) • Assessment (written tests if needed)	7. Question and answer session (Travel)

Materials Hardware: KW DC electric motors, control panels
        Control: Thyristor Leonardo (DSR)
            • ASR control
            • Field-magnet weakening control
            • Regenerative control
            • Isolated operation
            • Soft-start control
            • Sequential operation control
            • Pulse feedback control

Figure 7-10. Electrical Systems Maintenance Course A-2

8

TPM and the JIT
Production System

This chapter describes various schemes for speeding up the deployment of MQP management. The use of the JIT (just-in-time) production system is particularly effective in stepping up the pace because of its synergy with TPM.

Using JIT to organize operations so they all produce the right quantities at the right time is a decisive challenge. As a means of coping with high-variety, small-lot, short-lead-time production, it is a system that delivers untold benefits in terms of reduced lead times and slashed costs.

Based on the notion of making only the number of products required as they are sold, it aims to have every operation make the needed items at the right time and in the right quantities at low cost. To achieve this, each operation *pulls* exactly what it requires from the previous operation and makes exactly the amount pulled from it by the next operation. By making this the general practice throughout the factory, JIT pursues the goals of one-piece flow, small-lot leveled production, and inventory minimization. Implementing this system drastically decreases lead times and eliminates waste (in other words, cuts costs) by exposing latent problems (see Figure 8-1). And it has achieved wide recognition as a valuable production control system able to cope with the harshest business environment.

When described in these terms, it might seem as if any company that introduced JIT would be able to achieve fantastic results, but it actually takes tremendous determination and commitment to succeed.

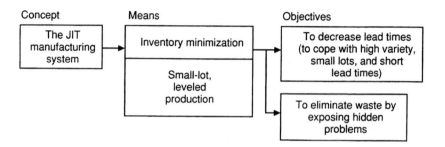

Figure 8-1. The Aims of the JIT Manufacturing System

The JIT system has already demonstrated its tremendous cost-cutting effect on automobile production lines and other mechanical processing and parts-assembly facilities. However, it is not so easy to introduce and develop in materials-processing plants. To ensure that all materials and parts flow through every stage of the production process according to the just-in-time principle, you must greatly increase the number of changeovers by drastically decreasing changeover times. You must also try to eliminate inventory through small-lot, leveled production. There is an almost infinite number of problems to be overcome to achieve this, including the need to eliminate defects. With respect to equipment, independent, isolated units are linked with conveyor lines, converting many operations into a continuous production line. Even when equipment cannot be moved, JIT attempts to eliminate work-in-process as if the separate units were connected (see Figure 8-2).

Conventional large-lot production

- Individual equipment items separated
- After a certain quantity has been made, it is taken to the next operation

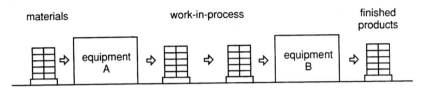

After improvement: small-lot production

- Equipment is centralized
- Goods are made one at a time

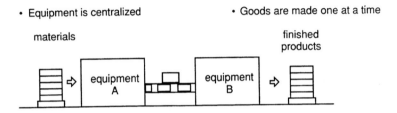

Figure 8-2. Streamlining Production Processes

DEPLOYMENT OF THE JIT PRODUCTION SYSTEM

A statement of intent by top executives, division, and department managers is also a prerequisite for the introduction of the JIT production system. They must want to challenge the limits of the possible and participate in the effort to effect a change.

The lowering of inventory levels brought about by this system reveals hidden problems and makes it essential to expedite improvements aimed at eliminating waste. Moreover, the JIT system must not be implemented unless a proper TPM foundation has been laid. Introducing and developing JIT at the same time as those activities described in the previous chapters is extremely effective, however. It creates a synergistic effect and greatly augments the results.

As mentioned, reducing inventory brings latent problems to the surface. However, people who accept the need to systematize and upgrade improvement skills will not be unduly inconvenienced by these problems. Instead, they will be able to forestall quality and delivery problems, producing excellent results.

It is essential to adopt a positive attitude and be ready to improve anything, no matter what the problem may be. For this purpose, statements of resolve by top executives and division and department managers at the introductory stage are vital to both TPM and JIT. They are the key to reforming people's attitudes and behavior.

PROBLEMS REVEALED BY JIT

The following problems commonly surface as inventory levels are lowered.

1. When equipment frequently breaks down or takes a long time to fix, in-process stocks are held in case the line stops. This provides a feeling of security. In a process plant, the equipment capacities of each operation are, in principle, balanced, and this results in large losses if the plant is shut down because of equipment failure. The fewer equipment units there are of the same type, the greater these losses and the larger the amount of in-process stock. However, the more equipment units there are, the more difficult it is to ensure the overall reliability of the line. This situation makes maintenance management very important and in some cases makes it the key to success or failure of production.

2. When there are many in-process quality defects, subsequent operations stop, delivery dates are missed, and there is an accumulation of surplus items and dead stock made in anticipation of rework. Rework produced to replace defective products has to be rushed through, and this also disrupts the process.

3. When operations are poorly connected, individual operations may be deluded into thinking that it is not

only more efficient, but also cheaper to make products in large batches. When this happens, work-in-process accumulates or the subsequent operations stop.

4. If it takes a long time to retool for producing different models, different sizes, etc., a large amount of work-in-process will build up, the next operation will stop, productivity will drop and loss rates will increase.

5. Work-in-process will always accumulate if a particular operation is more highly loaded than the others and forms a bottleneck in the line. This happens when the production capacity of the operation is unstable or cannot match the planned production volume. For example, work-in-process or completed products will accumulate if people make extra when the equipment for that particular operation is working well; or they will come in on their days off to catch up when other operations are shut down.

6. Work-in-process will build up if equipment is operated unnecessarily because people feel it wasteful to let expensive machinery sit idle. The same happens if people are made to produce more than is necessary because it is thought undesirable to allow them to do nothing.

7. Discipline is all-important. Without it, people will not be able to follow rules. As a result, things will not flow smoothly and work-in-process will build up. The work flow will also be adversely affected by poor maintenance practices and a low level of improvement awareness during routine management activities.

8. Accidents due to unsafe equipment or unsafe practices will have a greater direct effect on the overall production process after the introduction of JIT. It is important to be constantly on the alert and prevent accidents through prevention training.

9. A high absentee rate or frequent unexpected absences will adversely affect the process flow.

10. If there are few people with improvement ability in the workplace and the workplace lacks improvement muscle, improvements will come too late and operations will be disrupted. Small-lot production creates a need for a variety of improvements but exacerbates the bad effects of introducing them too slowly.

11. If workers lack skill or have not yet developed multiple skills, work-in-process will accumulate and subsequent operations will stop.

12. Processes will stop if subcontractors have insufficient capacity to meet delivery dates.

13. If large-lot production is continued because people are afraid of change, work-in-process will accumulate or subsequent operations will stop. To eliminate the waste arising from overproducing, things must be made to flow smoothly through the process. To do this, lots must be made as small as possible while meeting the production requirement for each product model. But people's defensive instinct often comes into play. Fearing that they might not be able to produce the required output, they make things in large lots, thus increasing the amount of work-in-process and other stocks. They then relax and enjoy the margin of safety they have created.

14. Long lead times mean that raw materials, work-in-process, and operating stocks pile up. These include transient raw materials and finished products left behind as a result of unofficial cancellations and changes. It also includes work-in-process laid aside to allow rush orders to be passed through, and forecast-based operating stocks which have to be held in large quantities because any sold are not replaced until the following month.

TPM ACTIVITIES NEEDED IN JIT

As discussed in the previous section, the greater the reduction in work-in-process and other stocks attendant on the promotion of the JIT production system, the more problems and wastes are brought to light (see Figure 8-3). This is invaluable. To recognize its worth and to address these problems, courage and confidence are essential. Overcoming all obstacles makes the development and upgrading of TPM an even more urgent task.

If TPM activities lack vitality, people will be concerned solely with clearing up problems after the event. This means that, while inventory may decrease to some extent, an insurmountable barrier will eventually be reached. JIT cannot be established without a foundation of TPM and other activities. However wonderful a production control system is introduced, it will be impossible to realize its true benefits if the ability to maintain and manage it is absent.

It is therefore tremendously valuable to introduce JIT after TPM has reached a certain level, while continuing to develop the latter. This approach will enhance the results achieved through TPM activities.

Implementing JIT requires a completely new way of thinking. This means that various problems are bound to occur when it is introduced on a full scale, even in factories that have carefully prepared for it. Do not, therefore, be put off by a certain amount of initial confusion; instead, bring the problems into the open and solve them. If these problems are steadily solved, inventory will dwindle visibly, while losses will decrease and multiskilling will lead to more efficient, enthusiastic workers. Introducing JIT heightens the need for some of the conditions and activities that TPM aims at. These are described in the following text.

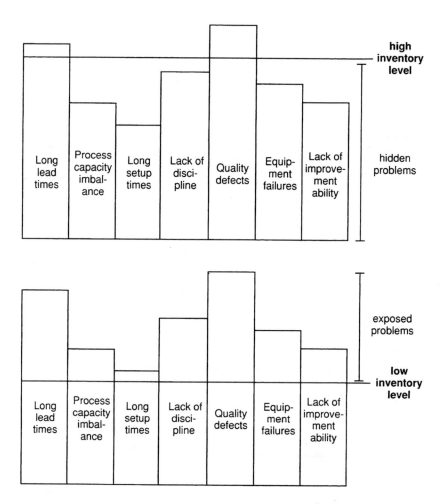

Figure 8-3. Low Inventory Exposes Problems to Address

Creating a Disciplined Workplace

Creating a milieu in which people are able to stick to what they or others have decided is indispensable for the deployment of both TPM and JIT. The greater the level of factory management, the more effort will be put into creating this kind of atmosphere, and the more important discipline will become.

The Five S's are introduced through a simple system in which everyone's role and share of responsibility are decided and simple activities in which everyone participates are started. This provides for basic activities that are easy to understand.

In TPM, you try to create a disciplined workplace by changing everybody's attitude and behavior through the practice of the Five S's. The significant feature about these activities is that people make a willing effort to adhere to standards they themselves have set. If a workplace cannot adhere to the Five S's according to the rules, there is no way it can adhere to work standards and other routine standards. This is why it is important to patiently and persistently inculcate the practice of these activities.

In practicing the Five S's and other types of corrective action and countermeasures, it is important to respond promptly to problems. Encourage the attitude that problems must be solved within a single day, through *One Is Best* and *One-Day Action* campaigns. When trouble occurs, countermeasures must be discussed immediately, and it is also effective to hold a meeting beside the machine the morning after the day on which trouble has occurred. At this meeting, the effects of improvement measures can be discussed, and for this the support of staff and superiors is indispensable. The Five S's must be implemented rapidly and thoroughly. Unfortunately, some factories do not understand the true significance of the Five S's and they get discouraged. However, the difference in results between factories that practice the Five S's halfheartedly and those that practice them conscientiously are unmistakable.

Building Efficient Production Lines

The JIT production system addresses the question of operation rates and demands that equipment be ready to start at any time in response to production requirements. As the ideal of stockless production is approached, try to ensure that equipment is highly reliable from startup to shutdown and that it always functions perfectly and never breaks down.

Before introducing JIT, when the focus is on developing TPM activities, there is often little need to reduce stoppage severity rates below approximately 0.1 percent. After introducing JIT, however, there may be a real, urgent need to improve this figure — and necessity is the mother of invention.

Improving the output operating rate. When process production capacities are unbalanced, a certain operation will form a bottleneck and work will build up behind it. You then must immediately improve the output operating rate for that operation. Also, if one particular operation works on a holiday during a busy period, a large amount of work-in-process will accumulate downstream of that operation on the morning after the holiday. This not only seriously obstructs the production flow, but also means that extra spools and containers are required for storing the products. This is why it is so important to increase the output operating rate of bottleneck operations. The need to start with such operations is obvious, and the effect of increasing their operating ratios will be great.

Shortening changeover times and reducing setup losses. Switching to small-lot production greatly multiplies the number of changeovers performed. To hold the overall changeover time and material losses below their existing values, it is necessary to reduce the time required for each changeover and to reduce the accompanying material loss. To do so requires a corresponding improvement in the workplace. At the same time, you must strive to increase the output operating rate.

Boosting output by small-lot production. Avoid raising the output operating rates of individual machines at the expense of small-lot production. Guard against making things in large lots (and consequently overproducing) to increase the apparent efficiency and output operating rates of individual operations. Producing in large lots, makes unsalable products and accumulates dead stocks. Whatever happens, your first duty is to raise output operating ratios as part of small-lot production. This approach will cut materials and labor and favorably affect profits.

Even on very busy production lines, decreasing in-process stocks will expose problems and waste. The improvements then instituted to deal with these will result in higher output operating ratios. This may be hard to understand at first, but seeing is believing — processes thought to be bottlenecks very often cease to be so. It is important to realize quickly that the conventional approach is wrong.

Increasing equipment speeds. Increased speeds help to increase process capacities but are counterproductive if they result in breakdowns and defects. Failure and defect rates are said to increase in proportion to the square of the factor by which the speed is multiplied. In practice, this means that equipment which frequently fails or produces defective products is often operated at below its intended speed. Before trying to raise speeds, it is therefore best to eliminate failures and defects and increase the reliability of the equipment. In the final analysis, this is the easiest way to increase capacity.

Output management. Normally, the production outputs that are planned for certain periods are calculated based on orders forecast for the month. These periods can include a day, one shift, or the entire planned production time which includes operating time, changeover time, inspection time, and miscellaneous time. These planned outputs are compared with the actual results as a routine management activity, and the need for improvement arises from differences between the two. Keep trying to get closer to the plans by making improvements and taking corrective action to ensure that actual production does not lag behind or creep ahead of planned production.

As the standard output per unit time, on which your production plans are based, do not take the average of past results but a figure which makes you try to match the previous best record.

Building Reliable Production Lines

Reducing work-in-process reveals hidden problems, while measures to decrease dead stocks limit the production of surplus products. To solve these problems, product quality must be built in through the equipment. The techniques that achieve this are TPM and MQP management. MQP management probes the relationships between product quality and the deterioration of equipment and processing conditions. In MQP management, there is a single-minded dedication to preventive quality maintenance. Activities include probing the quality-defect situation; identifying the parameters that affect product quality; pinpointing the processes, equipment parts, and processing conditions where these parameters are deficient and analyzing the factors that make them change; developing sensors and mistake-proofing devices for quality assurance, and devising action standards for hardware improvement and maintenance. If defects decrease, work-in-process will naturally also decrease, while the work flow will become more streamlined and there will be fewer quality complaints and claims.

To fulfill an order for 100 products, it is not uncommon for enough materials to be injected into the process to produce from 102 to 105. The extra materials are intended to cover the projected defective products, setup and adjustment losses. Since this is so obviously a loss, decide in future to commit the exact amount of materials required by each order, even if it means having to do another production run. Doing so will often change people's attitudes and eliminate the defects. Needless to say, production surpluses will also cease.

Developing Equipment-Competent People

The further JIT is taken, the greater the need for improvement. The speed of improvement is greatly affected by the ability to maintain equipment in its optimal state and implement effective improvement programs. This ability will be lacking in both quality and quantity if it is confined exclusively to maintenance personnel. Therefore, it is essential to utilize the strength of the production divisions with their large complements.

Under the JIT regime, efficiency is often improved by making operators responsible for several processes as part of streamlining production. This means taking operators away from simple, repetitive work and giving them the more complex task of multiprocess handling. This is a step in the direction of multiskilling. Operators must become knowledgeable about jigs, tools, dies, and other equipment. This will give them the maintenance and improvement skills required by JIT and enable them to perform routine maintenance and improvement activities such as measuring, analyzing, taking corrective action, performing minor repairs, servicing, and so on. If a company puts its heart into expanding its base of equipment-competent people through TPM over a period of five to ten years, it can easily create a management structure that no other company can match.

Mistake-proofing devices and jigs and tools designed to improve changeover often look simple when finished — but actually inventing them requires appropriate experience and training. To rely on the ingenuity of the shop floor to come up with the many improvements needed, it is imperative for operators to become conversant with the functions and construction of machinery, jigs, and tools. The best improvement suggestions are aimed at preventing quality defects or raising productivity by dealing with machinery, jigs, tools, mistake-proofing devices, and other equipment. These suggestions indicate that equipment-competent people are being developed in the workplace, and great importance must be attached to the creation of excellent equipment, jigs, etc. by the operators themselves.

Have factory workers form small improvement teams, participate in equipment improvement sessions, and actually carry out a variety of improvement work. This is an extremely positive policy, since joining an improvement team for a certain period helps people to rapidly acquire improvement and fabrication skills.

Improvement teams are also a way of coping with fluctuations in demand, since workers can be assigned to them at slack times and returned to the line during busy periods.

Building Production Lines with Character

Whether a process designed by linking separate items of equipment works well or not has long been said to depend largely on the thoroughness of the research performed before it comes off the drawing board. The methodology of this has been investigated in the guise of management systems such as MP (maintenance-prevention) design and CD (cost-down) design. Even so, process capacities are surprisingly often unbalanced, and there is regret for the obvious wasted investment in equipment. Some plants that appear at first sight to be highly automated, are actually mountains of waste. Because there are often too many conveyors and excessive amounts of work-in-process, streamlining improvements are instituted in an attempt to reduce work-in-process and boost the capacity of high-load lines. However, these improvements are instituted after the equipment has been set up, and may include such things as removing conveyors just installed between operations and totally revamping equipment layouts to facilitate the production process.

When planning and designing new equipment, engineers must concern themselves with equipment technology as well as purchasing technology. They must accumulate basic research aimed at producing real increases in productivity, cost cuts, and quality assurance; they must identify all types of waste, and build their findings into the equipment in tangible form. At the equipment and process-design stage, engineers must not only review their past methods and pay attention to process-automation rates and production capacities but also consider ways of making the equipment easier to operate and less wasteful.

Although the engineers may agree with what they are told, incorporating innovations at the new equipment planning stage is not easy from either the technical or the cost viewpoint. It needs considerable experience and ingenuity together with the correct data, and engineers should use hands-on improvement sessions to study existing equipment. Items that cannot be dealt with at the planning and design stages are thoroughly analyzed for deficiencies at the early equipment management stage. In addition, operating procedures and maintenance standards are perfected, and a sound basis is established for future PM methods. Nevertheless, the proper operation of new machinery and ideal equipment conditions often remain obscure and upset production with unexpected breakdowns and chronic defects.

In addition, there is a movement away from the "big-gun" plant used in the mass-production era toward equipment suitable for flexible, small-lot production. Equipment is changing to allow processing conditions to be altered easily, to do away with adjustments, to accomplish setup rapidly by methods such as "one-touch setup" (while minimizing losses when this is done), and to make work flow smoothly.

INCREASING THE SPEED OF IMPROVEMENTS

To cope with changes in the current situation, with its harsh environment and rapid pace of technological innovation, a company's constitution must be made stronger. To do so, it is necessary to reject long-established customs and harmful practices by revolutionizing people's attitudes and behavior and accelerating the rate of improvements and reforms such as the development of MQP management. With a foundation of effective routine management, you can use equipment improvement sessions and other approaches to immediately realize results that would be expected to take months or years with the old way of thinking.

A Sense of Urgency

Without a sense of crisis, there will be no commitment and conviction. Without commitment and conviction, there will be

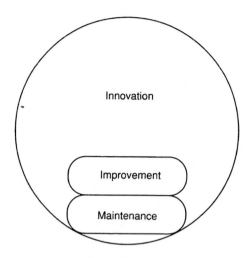

**Figure 8-4. Innovation, Improvement
and Maintenance**

no action. Factory reform requires that a sense of crisis be felt throughout the organization, right down to individual workers. Information from customers, comparisons with competitors, and the knowledge of local shortcomings and problems communicated this sense of urgency to all. It is hard to impart a sense of urgency when things are going well, but this is the very time when it should be done, with references to the future. For example:

- Exports are unlikely to increase in the future, while the outlook for domestic demand is unstable
- Imports of low-added-value products from the newly industrialized economies will increase rapidly from now on
- We have to create an organization that will allow us to survive even when operating at 70 percent of our present capacity
- Orders will dry up unless we reduce our cost prices by 20 percent a year
- Our future will be bleak if we allow our competitors to outperform us

Pursuing the Ideal

In TPM, you pursue the ideal state of equipment. But the pursuit of the ideal should not be confined to equipment alone. Each individual, each workplace, and the company as a whole must aim at perfection. It is vital that company policy runs like an unbroken thread through all levels of the organization. Within the cycle of policy management, each individual and workplace must have a goal to which to aspire, the desire to attain it, and the satisfaction of achieving it.

Changing Behavior

By reducing the number of people, machines, and materials, improvements are made more efficiently and skillfully and the level of management is raised.

Work-in-process and warehouse stocks serve to hide waste and problems. If nothing is done about them, waste will continue to be ignored and the factory will decline into a sorry state with a low level of management. This is why the JIT system is so cunning: By eliminating inventory and thereby making waste and problems more visible, it aims to shock us into making rapid improvements.

It is often said that too many cooks spoil the broth. Try to make early cuts in the number of workers attending the equipment as soon as it appears feasible, pulling people out and assigning them to maintenance, other areas, or improvement teams. The scarcity of workers helps make improvement imperative.

By refraining from installing extra equipment when demand increases and by mothballing idle equipment when demand is low, make it essential to increase output operating ratios.

Equipment Improvement Sessions

As described in the first section of Chapter 7, hold intensive one-day equipment improvement sessions designed to produce immediate results. These sessions are carried out by groups whose members include specialists and division and department managers from other divisions, and are intended to support the routine management activities performed by the standing organization and small groups.

When problems which cannot be solved by normal management or small group activities are tackled in equipment improvement sessions, a flurry of activity takes place over a single day. Everyone abandons their preconceptions and pools their knowledge and ingenuity to cut through the blocks and achieve quick results. Skillfully putting people on the spot like this brings out their best ideas and the best type of action. Holding these sessions periodically and taking an approach to improvement that is as positive as possible gradually changes everyone's attitudes.

Using Outside Help

When customers or people from other companies come to visit or study your factory, regard this as a valuable opportunity to solicit their opinions and advice. Having people see what you are doing, ask about it, and point things out helps step up the pace of improvement. Praise from outsiders encourages a redoubling of efforts in the future, while criticism helps point out problems for future improvement.

BASIC BEHAVIORAL INDICATORS ON THE ROAD TO IMPROVEMENT

The preceding sections have discussed some schemes for quickening the improvement tempo, but the fundamental quest is to change people's attitudes toward improvement and reform their behavior so that they enjoy taking up a challenge.

Enthusiasm at going for goals. Top-flight consultants may be employed, but they cannot do the work for you. The enthusiasm and motivation of the people in each division are essential.

Developments which permeate to every part of the organization can only be achieved if everyone works cooperatively with commitment and persistence. "Ten heads are better than one."

Shatter the status quo. Do you have a narrow view of the world, like a frog down a well? Are you sure you have not become a self-satisfied, blinkered specialist? Be bold enough to try breaking down the old thought-patterns and myths which give such a false sense of confidence. New ways of looking at things and novel methods are born when present methods are regarded as the worst possible and the status quo is shattered by changing everything. Improvement starts with the courage to demand change.

Establish priorities. There are many kinds of waste in the workplace, presenting a host of valuable opportunities for improvement. There is a tendency to shuffle around blindly without recognizing waste for what it is or blaming it all on someone else. To overcome this, make waste visible immediately. Division and department managers must take the lead in developing people's faculty for spotting waste and actively try to observe, analyze, judge, and tackle problems. Close attention must also be paid to factors which hinder people from doing what they should. It is particularly important to allocate time for autonomous maintenance, inspection, education and small-group activities.

Respect experimental measures. Give more importance to rough-and-ready, low-cost solutions than elaborate, time-consuming schemes. If a plan yields disappointing results, be prepared to change it immediately. Too much theorizing and planning makes it difficult to come to grips with problems and creates long delays before improvements are effected. Dare to put ideas into action right away, without spending money, by experimenting and testing with makeshift equipment. Respect the simple, quick response, and promote this attitude with slogans such as:

- If something is dirty, clean it the same day

- When a problem occurs, deal with it the same day
- When getting things out, take out three items in one minute
- Wind up meetings within one hour

Don't make excuses. Act! Avoid dragging up the past by saying things like, "We tried that before and it didn't work", "We're doing the best we can", and "That's too difficult — it can't be done." Rather than talk about what happened in the past, think about how to make things work in the future. The more excuses a workplace finds, the less enthusiastic it is about improvement. Before hunting for reasons for not attempting something, be prepared to listen carefully to what others have to say, believe in them, and follow their advice.

Support the enthusiastic attitude that makes people say such things as, "If I don't improve things, who will?" and "If we don't do it now when we're so busy, when on earth will we find time to do it?" Discourage moaning at others with comments such as, "Our new workers are so unskilled these days," "The equipment is always breaking down," "Our partner companies are letting us down," "We're constantly busy sorting out problems," and "We can't practice PM because we don't get enough support from the staff." Start by doing what you can.

People often wriggle out of making improvements by promising to start when they have time. And when they eventually do have time, they get out of it again with excuses such as, "We don't have enough people," "The equipment isn't working," "We can't whip up any enthusiasm," "Improvements won't have much effect," and "We can't spend any money." It's little wonder that divisions like this often can't even list the problems they face during high-load periods.

Busy periods are the very times to introduce improvements, and a little effort will produce terrific results.

Respond to change. An organization cannot be said to be truly capable if problems arise when the load increases slightly and it cannot cope with the extra burden. Real progress will only have been made when it can respond to variations in both quantity and quality of production.

Self-reflection. When performing maintenance or instituting preventive measures, give importance not just to completing equipment or system improvements but also to changing people's attitudes and behavior. Review what has been done and summarize points to reflect on, observations and things you are proud of. This leads to the next round of improvements and helps keep everyone enthusiastic.

Quality first. To win the trust of customers, the next process and salespeople, *quality first* must be the basis of plant management.

Safety first. It is particularly important to check the safety of the workplace after effecting improvements.

9

Improvement Results and
Future Topics

Creating perfect, defect-free production lines has been a particularly popular topic in recent years, and is becoming more and more important. Manufacturers have discovered that improving quality means that things cost less to make — and they are now claiming that good quality equals low cost. Profitable operation is impossible if losses such as defective products, scrap, etc. are created because of large variations in processing conditions or quality-component accuracy. The better the quality of the product, the lower its cost, and we should even be able to say that a product is of high quality if it is made cheaply. Sharpening abilities through the zero-defect challenge makes activities designed to increase productivity or reduce inventory easy.

THE RESULTS OF DEPLOYING MQP MANAGEMENT

TPM has been developed in many factories belonging to Furukawa Electric and its affiliates, and MQP management techniques have been employed to eliminate defects from the production processes. As a result, many examples can be cited in which this has not only reduced failures (i.e., stoppage severity rates) and slashed defect rates but has also helped greatly to save energy and improve indicators such as the output operating rate (see Figures 9-1 to 9-3).

The fact that Furukawa Electric's overseas affiliates have also achieved outstanding results deserves particular mention, and Figure 9-4 shows an example of this.

Deploying MQP management with conviction and tenacity is bound to give results wherever it is applied. It drastically reduces both visible and hidden defects, and yields a variety of intangible benefits, some of which are:

- Overcoming resistance to change in the workplace
- Increased customer confidence
- Heightened morale and re-energized small-group activities.

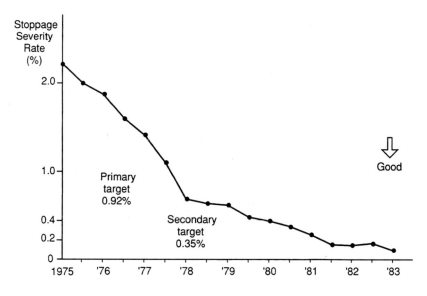

Figure 9-1. Trend in Equipment Stoppage Severity Rate

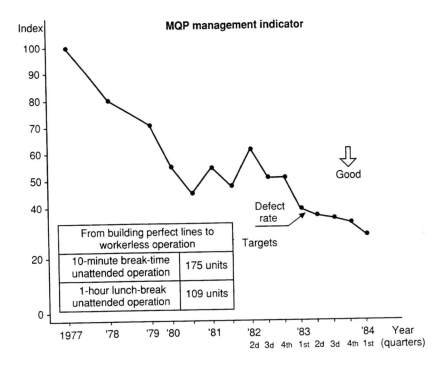

Figure 9-2. Trend in Defect Rate Index

- Progress in developing human capacities, e.g., creating a base for multiskilling
- Laying the foundation for the development of activities other than TPM

BUILDING NEW EQUIPMENT WITH SPECIAL FEATURES

It is important to continue trying to make improvements to equipment that make it even more of a pleasure to operate. To do this, Furukawa Electric is taking the information and know-how obtained through MQP management on existing equipment and feeding it back into the development of new equipment from the design stage on, by practicing MP design, for example.

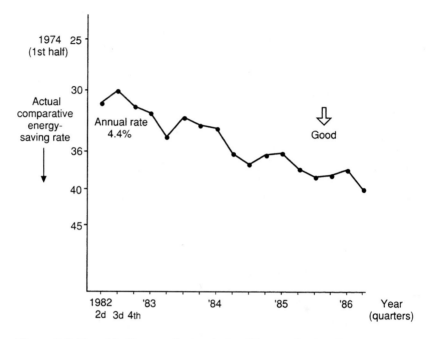

Figure 9-3. Trend in Energy-Saving Index (Energy-Saving Rate)

As for early equipment management, we tend to identify the quality components and manage their maintenance at every stage (fabrication, installation, test operation, and adjustment). When problems are discovered, these will be listed and dealt with as promptly as possible through improvement and education. When more rework and adjustment are required than expected, try to find out why this has happened, what improvements can be effected, and what methods are available for predicting a recurrence of the same abnormality. This information on to the next round of design.

In this way, we hope to avoid becoming slaves to high technology. Active feedback of improvement information obtained from deficiencies in existing equipment will help us create original new equipment that will truly delight the operators.

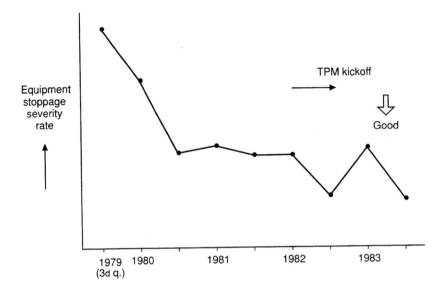

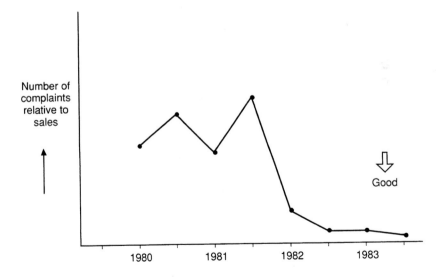

Figure 9-4. Results Achieved by Overseas Affiliates

THE IMPORTANCE OF TECHNOLOGY

As equipment becomes more complex and computerized, specific technologies for processing, maintenance, and diagnosis are growing in importance daily. However, there will not be as much improvement in these areas as hoped for if the need for it is not made apparent. TPM and MQP management revealed this need and made it essential to understand equipment and processing mechanisms by fully utilizing equipment technology and proprietary technology. The need is increasing for computer-aided maintenance and diagnostic technology, and these areas are being constantly researched.

About the Author

In 1956, Seiji Tsuchiya was graduated from the Mechanical Engineering Department of the No. 1 Faculty of Science and Engineering of Waseda University. The same year, he joined Furukawa Electric, where he became responsible for equipment design, planning, and maintenance work. In 1969, he was appointed engineering department manager at Furukawa's Chiba Works. Mr. Tsuchiya has worked since 1978 to develop and establish TPM, QC, and JIT on the factory floor. Currently, he gives guidance and support to Furukawa's many factories and affiliates in his role as division manager responsible for the Production Efficiency Promoting Group. TPM is a key activity of this group, and Mr. Tsuchiya has a reputation for sharing practical guidance on this subject. Mr. Tsuchiya is also an active leader of seminars and study missions and a contributor to technical journals.

Index

Deterioration, equipment,
    97-98, 149-52
Dirt, 95

Early equipment
    management, 194
Education. *See* Training
Employees
    maintenance skills of,
        xvii-iii, 4, 7-8, 181
    participation by, xix, 4, 29,
        101-3
    training of, 80-89
    and work environment, xii
Equipment, 6-7, 9, 13, 164, 179
    accuracy of, 160-61
    building, 193-94
    failure of, 91-99
    improvements in, 11, 110,
        117-18, 125-30, 185-86
    maintaining, 3, 120-25,
        150-51
Equipment consciousness,
    86-87
Equipment-directed
    management, 5

Failure, equipment, 91-99
Failure-rate curve, 92-93
Fittings, tightening, 47-52
Five S's, 20, 177
    definition of, 31-32
    follow up in, 43-44
    goals of, 32-36

implementing, 36-42
    and next steps, 44-46
Furukawa, Ichibee, 15
Furukawa Electric, xii, 15-17
    JIT at, xiv, 22-25
    MQP management at,
        191-93
    TPM deployment at, xi,
        18-22

Hardware solutions, xi

Identification chart, 130-35
Idling, eliminating, 157-60
Improvement, 43, 118-20, 182
    behavioral principles of,
        186-89
    choosing activities for, 23-25
    equipment, 11, 110, 117-18,
        125-30
    implementing, 111-13
    increasing speed of, 183-86
Inspection, 2, 27, 59-66, 75, 145
Inventory, reducing, 171-72

Japan Institute of Plant
    Engineers (JIPE), 4
JIT, 169-71, 185
    deployment of, 171-74
    at Furukawa Electric, xiv,
        22-25
    and TPM, xiv, 175-83

Kaizen, xix
Kanban, 70

BOOKS FROM PRODUCTIVITY PRESS

Productivity Press publishes books that empower individuals and companies to achieve excellence in quality, productivity, and the creative involvement of all employees. Through steadfast efforts to support the vision and strategy of continuous improvement, Productivity Press delivers today's leading-edge tools and techniques gathered directly from industry leaders around the world. Call toll-free 1-800-394-6868 for our free catalog.

5 Pillars of the Visual Workplace
The Sourcebook for 5S Implementation
Hiroyuki Hirano

In this important sourcebook, JIT expert Hiroyuki Hirano provides the most vital information available on the visual workplace. He describes the 5Ss: in Japanese they are seiri, seiton, seiso, seiketsu, and shitsuke (which translate as organization, orderliness, cleanliness, standardized cleanup, and discipline). Hirano discusses how the 5S theory fosters efficiency, maintenance, and continuous improvement in all areas of the company, from the plant floor to the sales office. Presented in a thorough, detailed style, *5 Pillars of the Visual Workplace* explains why the 5Ss are important and the who, what, where, and how of 5S implementation. This book includes numerous case studies, hundreds of graphic illustrations, and over forty 5S user forms and training materials.
ISBN 1-56327-047-1 / 353 pages, illustrated / $85.00 / Order FIVE-B223

20 Keys to Workplace Improvement (Revised Edition)
Iwao Kobayashi

The 20 Keys system does more than just bring together twenty of the world's top manufacturing improvement approaches—it integrates these individual methods into a closely interrelated system for revolutionizing every aspect of your manufacturing organization. This revised edition of Kobayashi's best-seller amplifies the synergistic power of raising the levels of all these critical areas simultaneously. The new edition presents upgraded criteria for the five-level scoring system in most of the 20 Keys, supporting your progress toward becoming not only best in your industry but best in the world. New material and an updated layout throughout assist managers in implementing this comprehensive approach. In addition, valuable case studies describe how Morioka Seiko (Japan) advanced in Key 18 (use of microprocessors) and how Windfall Products (Pennsylvania) adapted the 20 Keys to its situation with good results.
ISBN 1-56327-109-5/ 312 pages / $50.00 / Order 20KREV- B223

PRODUCTIVITY PRESS, DEPT. BK, P.O. BOX 13390, PORTLAND, OR 97213-0390
Telephone: 1-800-394-6868   Fax: 1-800-394-6286

Achieving Total Quality Management
A Program for Action
Michel Perigord

This is an outstanding book on total quality management (TQM)—a compact guide to the concepts, methods, and techniques involved in achieving total quality. It shows you how to make TQM a companywide strategy, not just in technical areas, but in marketing and administration as well. Major methods and tools for total quality are spelled out and implementation strategies are reviewed.
ISBN 0-915299-60-7 / 392 pages / $50.00 / Order ACHTQM- B223

The Benchmarking Management Guide
American Productivity & Quality Center

If you're planning, organizing, or actually undertaking a benchmarking program, you need the most authoritative source of information to help you get started and to manage the process all the way through. Written expressly for managers of benchmarking projects by the APQC's renowned International Benchmarking Clearinghouse, this guide provides exclusive information from members who have already paved the way. It includes information on training courses and ways to apply Baldrige, Deming, and ISO 9000 criteria for internal assessment, and has a complete bibliography of benchmarking literature.
ISBN 1-56327-045-5 / 260 pages / $40.00 / Order BMG- B223

Corporate Diagnosis
Setting the Global Standard for Excellence
Thomas L. Jackson with Constance E. Dyer

All too often, strategic planning neglects the essential first and final steps: diagnosis of the organization's current state. What's required is a systematic review of the critical factors in organizational learning and growth, factors that require monitoring, measurement, and management to ensure that your company competes successfully. This executive workbook provides a step-by-step method for diagnosing an organization's strategic health and measuring its overall competitiveness against world class standards. With checklists, charts, and detailed explanations, *Corporate Diagnosis* is a practical instruction manual. The pillars of Jackson's diagnostic system are strategy, structure, and capability. Detailed diagnostic questions in each area are provided as guidelines for developing your own self-assessment survey.
ISBN 1-56327-086-2 / 100 pages / $65.00 / Order CDIAG- B223

PRODUCTIVITY PRESS, DEPT. BK, P.O. BOX 13390, PORTLAND, OR 97213-0390
Telephone: 1-800-394-6868   Fax: 1-800-394-6286

Equipment Planning for TPM
Maintenance Prevention Design
Fumio Gotoh

This practical book for design engineers, maintenance technicians, and manufacturing managers details a systematic approach to the improvement of equipment development and design and product manufacturing. The author analyzes five basic conditions for factory equipment of the future: development, reliability, economics, availability, and maintainability. The book's revolutionary concepts of equipment design and development enables managers to reduce equipment development time, balance maintenance and equipment planning and improvement, and improve quality production equipment.
ISBN 0-915299-77-1 / 337 pages / $85.00 / Order ETPM- B223

Feedback Toolkit
16 Tools for Better Communication in the Workplace
Rick Maurer

In companies striving to reduce hierarchy and foster trust and responsible participation, good person-to-person feedback can be as important as sophisticated computer technology in enabling effective teamwork. Feedback is an important map of your situation, a way to tell whether you are "on or off track." Used well, feedback can motivate people to their highest level of performance. Despite its significance, this level of information sharing makes most managers uncomfortable. *Feedback Toolkit* addresses this natural hesitation with an easy-to-grasp six-step framework and 16 practical and creative approaches for giving and receiving feedback with individuals and groups. Maurer's reality-tested methods in *Feedback Toolkit* are indispensable equipment for managers and teams in every organization.
ISBN 1-56327-056-0 / 109 pages / $12.00 / Order FEED- B223

Fast Focus on TQM
A Concise Guide to Companywide Learning
Derm Barrett

Finally, here's one source for all your TQM questions. Compiled in this concise, easy-to-read handbook are definitions and detailed explanations of over 160 key terms used in TQM. Organized in a simple alphabetical glossary form, the book can be used either as a primer for anyone being introduced to TQM or as a complete reference guide. It helps to align teams, departments, or entire organizations in a common understanding and use of TQM terminology. For anyone entering or currently involved in TQM, this is one resource you must have.
ISBN 1-56327-049-8 / 186 pages / $20.00 / Order FAST- B223

PRODUCTIVITY PRESS, DEPT. BK, P.O. BOX 13390, PORTLAND, OR 97213-0390
Telephone: 1-800-394-6868   Fax: 1-800-394-6286

Handbook for Productivity Measurement and Improvement
William F. Christopher and Carl G. Thor, eds.

An unparalleled resource! In over 100 chapters, nearly 80 front-runners in the quality movement reveal the evolving theory and specific practices of world class organizations. Spanning a wide variety of industries and business sectors, they discuss quality and productivity in manufacturing, service industries, profit centers, administration, nonprofit and government institutions, health care and education. Contributors include Robert C. Camp, Peter F. Drucker, Jay W. Forrester, Joseph M. Juran, Robert S. Kaplan, John W. Kendrick, Yasuhiro Monden, and Lester C. Thurow. Comprehensive in scope and organized for easy reference, this compendium belongs in every company and academic institution concerned with business and industrial viability.
ISBN 1-56327-007-2 / 1344 pages / $90.00 / Order HPM- B223

The Hunters and the Hunted
A Non-Linear Solution for Reengineering the Workplace
James B. Swartz

Our competitive environment changes rapidly. If you want to survive, you have to stay on top of those changes. Otherwise, you become prey to your competitors. Hunters continuously change and learn. Anyone who doesn't becomes the hunted and sooner or later will be devoured. This unusual non-fiction novel provides a veritable crash course in continuous transformation. It offers lessons from real-life companies and introduces many industrial gurus as characters. *The Hunters and the Hunted* doesn't simply tell you how to change tion novel provides a veritable crash course in continuous transformation. it offers lessons from real-life companies and introduces many industrial gurus as characters. *The Hunters and the Hunted* doesn't simply tell you how to change—it puts you inside the change process itself.
ISBN 1-56327-043-9 / 582 pages / $45.00 / Order HUNT- B223

The Idea Book
Improvement Through TEI (Total Employee Involvement)
Japan Human Relations Association

At last, a book showing how to create Total Employee Involvement (TEI) and get hundreds of ideas from each employee every year to improve every aspect of your organization. Gathering improvement ideas from your entire workforce is a must for global competitiveness. *The Idea Book,* heavily illustrated, is a hands-on teaching tool for workers and supervisors to refer to again and again. Perfect for study groups, too.
ISBN 0-915299-22-4 / 232 pages / $55.00 / Order IDEA- B223

Implementing a Lean Management System
Thomas L. Jackson with Karen R. Jones

Does your company think and act ahead of technological change, ahead of the customer, and ahead of the competition? Thinking strategically requires a company to face these questions with a clear future image of itself. *Implementing a Lean Management System* lays out a comprehensive management system for aligning the firm's vision of the future with market realities. Based on hoshin management —the Japanese strategic planning method used by top managers for driving TQM throughout an organization— Lean Management is about deploying vision, strategy, and policy to all levels of daily activity. It is a practical methodology emerging out of the implementation of continuous improvement methods and employee involvement. The key tools of this book builds on the knowledge of the worker, multiskilling, and an understanding of the role and responsibilities of the new lean manufacturer.
ISBN 1-56327-085-4 / 182 pages / $65.00 / Order ILMS- B223

Implementing TPM
The North American Experience
Charles J. Robinson and Andrew P. Ginder

The authors document an approach to TPM planning and deployment that modifies the JIPM 12-step process to accommodate the experiences of North American plants. They include details and advice on specific deployment steps, OEE calculation methodology, and autonomous maintenance deployment. This book shows how to make TPM work in unionized plants and how to position TPM to support and complement other strategic manufacturing improvement initiatives.
ISBN 1-56327-087-0 / 224 pages / $45.00 / Order IMPTPM- B223

Introduction to TPM
Total Productive Maintenance
Seiichi Nakajima

Total Productive Maintenance (TPM) combines preventive maintenance with Japanese concepts of total quality control (TQC) and total employee involvement (TEI). The result is a new system for equipment maintenance that optimizes effectiveness, eliminates breakdowns, and promotes autonomous operator maintenance through day-to-day activities. Here are the steps involved in TPM and case examples from top Japanese plants.
ISBN 0-915299-23-2 / 149 pages / $45.00 / Order ITPM- B223

PRODUCTIVITY PRESS, DEPT. BK, P.O. BOX 13390, PORTLAND, OR 97213-0390
Telephone: 1-800-394-6868   Fax: 1-800-394-6286

ISO 9000 REQUIRED
Your Worldwide Passport to Customer Confidence
Branimir Todorov

ISO 90000 certification is the required passport for suppliers who want to do global business today, and this book tells what you must do to qualify for it. Much has been written about implementation of ISO 9000, from detailed handbooks to full-length works focusing on a single aspect such as documentation. Todorov's *ISO 90000 Required* fills the need for a compact and readable guide for managers to the basics of ISO. Avoiding confusing and unnecessary details, the book is a valuable primer for managers looking for a basic introduction to the ISO standards, as well as an accessible reference to key topics for readers already involved in ISO certification.
ISBN 1-56327-112-5 / 211 pages, illustrated / $27.00 / Order ISOREQ- B223

Learning Organizations
Developing Cultures for Tomorrow's Workplace
Sarita Chawla and John Renesch, Editors

The ability to learn faster than your competition may be the only sustainable competitive advantage! A learning organization is one where people continually expand their capacity to create results they truly desire, where new and expansive patterns of thinking are nurtured, where collective aspiration is set free, and where people are continually learning how to learn together. This compilation of 34 powerful essays, written by recognized experts worldwide, is rich in concept and theory as well as application and example. An inspiring follow-up to Peter Senge's groundbreaking bestseller *The Fifth Discipline*, these essays are grouped in four sections that address all aspects of learning organizations: the guiding ideas behind systems thinking; the theories, methods, and processes for creating a learning organization; the infrastructure of the learning model; and arenas of practice.
ISBN 1-56327-110-9 / 575 pages / $35.00 / Order LEARN- B223

The Right Fit
The Power of Ergonomics as a Competitive Strategy
Clifford M. Gross

Each year, poorly designed products and workplaces account for thousands of injuries and skyrocketing costs. That's why ergonomics—the human factor in product and workplace design—is fast becoming a major concern of manufacturers. Now one of the country's top experts argues that ergonomics will become the next strategic imperative for American business, the deciding factor in which companies ultimately succeed. Here's a brilliant non-technical introduction for corporate planners and strategic decision makers.
ISBN 1-56327-111-7 / 185 pages / $24.00 / Order RIGHT- B223

PRODUCTIVITY PRESS, DEPT. BK, P.O. BOX 13390, PORTLAND, OR 97213-0390
Telephone: 1-800-394-6868   Fax: 1-800-394-6286

Making the Numbers Count
The Management Account as Change Agent on the World Class Team
Brian H. Maskell

Traditional accounting systems are holding back improvement strategies and process innovation. Maskell's timely book addresses the growing phenomenon confronting managers in continuous improvement environment. It unmasks the shortcomings of management accountants traditional roles and shows the inadequacy of running a business based on financial reports. According to Maskell, in a world class organization, the management accountant can and should take the lead in establishing performance measures that make a difference. Empowering frontline workers and middle managers to effectively improve their operations is one way to do it. Maskell provides the information management accountants need to become team members, leaders, and real innovators in their organizations.
ISBN: 1-56327-070-6 / 150 pages, illustrations / $29.00 / Order MNC- B223

Management for Quality Improvement
The 7 New QC Tools
Shigeru Mizuno, ed.

Building on the traditional seven QC tools, these tools were developed specifically for managers. They help in planning, troubleshooting, and communicating with maximum effectiveness at every stage of a quality improvement program and are certain to advance quality improvement efforts for anyone involved in project management, quality assurance, MIS, or TQC.
ISBN 0-915299-29-1 / 323 pages / $65.00 / Order 7QC- B223

Performance Measurement for World Class Manufacturing
A Model for American Companies
Brian H. Maskell

If your company is adopting world class manufacturing techniques, you'll need new methods of performance measurement to control production variables. In practical terms, this book describes the new methods of performance measurement and how they are used in a changing environment. For manufacturing managers as well as cost accountants, it provides a theoretical foundation of these innovative methods supported by extensive practical examples. The book specifically addresses performance measures for delivery, process time, production flexibility, quality, and finance.
ISBN 0-915299-99-2 / 448 pages / $55.00 / Order PERFM- B223

PRODUCTIVITY PRESS, DEPT. BK, P.O. BOX 13390, PORTLAND, OR 97213-0390
Telephone: 1-800-394-6868   Fax: 1-800-394-6286

Poka-Yoke
Improving Product Quality by Preventing Defects
Nikkan Kogyo Shimbun Ltd. and Factory Magazine (ed.)

If your goal is 100 percent zero defects, here is the book for you—a completely illustrated guide to poka-yoke (mistake-proofing) for supervisors and shop-floor workers. Many poka-yoke devices come from line workers and are implemented with the help of engineering staff. The result is better product quality—and increased participation by workers in efforts to improve your processes, your products, and your company as a whole.
ISBN 0-915299-31-3 / 295 pages / $65.00 / Order IPOKA- B223

A Revolution in Manufacturing
The SMED System
Shigeo Shingo

The heart of JIT is quick changeover methods. Dr. Shingo, inventor of the Single-Minute Exchange of Die (SMED) system for Toyota, shows you how to reduce your changeovers by an average of 98 percent! By applying Shingo's techniques, you'll see rapid improvements (lead time reduced from weeks to days, lower inventory and warehousing costs) that will improve quality, productivity, and profits.
ISBN 0-915299-03-8 / 383 pages / $80.00 / Order SMED- B223

Secrets of a Successful Employee Recognition System
Daniel C. Boyle

As the human resource manager of a failing manufacturing plant, Dan Boyle was desperate to find a way to motivate employees and break down the barrier between management and the union. He came up with a simple idea to say thank you to you employees for doing their job. In *Secrets to a Successful Employee Recognition System*, Boyle outlines how to begin and run a 100 Club program. Filled with case studies and detailed guidelines, this book underscores the power behind thanking your employees for a job well done.
ISBN 1-56327-083-8 / 250 pages / $25.00 / Order SECRET- B223

Stepping Up to ISO 14000
Integrating Environmental Quality with ISO 9000 and TQM
Subash C. Puri

The newest ISO standards, announced in mid-1996, require environmentally-friendly practices in every aspect of a manufacturing business, from factory design and raw material acquisition to the production, packaging, distribution, and ultimate disposal of the product. Hereís a comprehensible overview and implementation guide to the standards thatís also the only one to show how they fit with current ISO 9000 efforts and other companywide programs for Total Quality Management (TQM).
ISBN 1-56327-129-X / 280 pages / $39.00 / Order SPTISO- B223

PRODUCTIVITY PRESS, DEPT. BK, P.O. BOX 13390, PORTLAND, OR 97213-0390
Telephone: 1-800-394-6868   Fax: 1-800-394-6286

Toyota Production System
Beyond Large-Scale Production
Taiichi Ohno

Here's the first information ever published in Japan on the Toyota production system (known as Just-In-Time manufacturing). Here Ohno, who created JIT for Toyota, reveals the origins, daring innovations, and ceaseless evolution of the Toyota system into a full management system. You'll learn how to manage JIT from the man who invented it, and to create a winning JIT environment in your own manufacturing operation.
ISBN 0-915299-14-3 / 162 pages / $45.00 / Order OTPS- B223

TPM for America
What It Is and Why You Need It
Herbert R. Steinbacher and Norma L. Steinbacher

As much as 15 to 40 percent of manufacturing costs are attributable to maintenance. With a fully implemented TPM program, your company can eradicate all but a fraction of these costs. Co-written by an American TPM practitioner and an experienced educator, this book gives a convincing account of why American companies must adopt TPM if we are to successfully compete in world markets. Includes examples from leading American companies showing how TPM has changed them.
ISBN 1-56327-044-7 / 169 pages / $25.00 / Order TPMAM- B223

TPM Team Guide
Kunio Shirose (ed.)

This book makes TPM team activities understandable to everyone in the company.*TPM Team Guide* gives simple explanations of basic TPM concepts like the 6 big losses, and emphasizes the integration of TPM activities with production management. Chapters describe the team-based improvement process step by step, from goal setting to standardization of the improved operations. Team leaders will learn how to hold effective meetings and work with the human issues that are a big part of success. The tools for team problem solving and the steps for preparing a good presentation of results are detailed here as well. Written in straightforward, easy to digest language, with abundant illustrations and cartoon examples. Frontline supervisors, operators, facilitators, and trainers in manufacturing companies will want to use this practical guide to improve company performance and build a satisfying workplace for employees.
ISBN 1-56327-079-X/175 pages / $25.00 / Order TGUIDE- B223

PRODUCTIVITY PRESS, DEPT. BK, P.O. BOX 13390, PORTLAND, OR 97213-0390
Telephone: 1-800-394-6868   Fax: 1-800-394-6286

The Unshackled Organization
Facing the Challenge of Unpredictability Through Spontaneous Reorganization
Jeffrey Goldstein

Managers should not necessarily try to solve all the internal problems within their organizations. Intervention may help in the short term, but in the long run may inhibit true problem-solving change from taking place. And change is the real goal. Through change comes real hope for improvement. Using leading-edge scientific and social theories about change, Goldstein explores how change happens within an organization and reveals that only through "self-organization" can natural, lasting change occur. This book is a pragmatic guide for managers, executives, consultants, and other change agents. ISBN 1-56327-048-X / 208 pages / $25.00 / Order UO- B223

TO ORDER: Write, phone, or fax Productivity Press, Dept. BK, P.O. Box 13390, Portland, OR 97213-0390, phone 1-800-394-6868, fax 1-800-394-6286. Send check or charge to your credit card (American Express, Visa, MasterCard accepted).

U.S. ORDERS: Add $5 shipping for first book, $2 each additional for UPS surface delivery. Add $5 for each AV program containing 1 or 2 tapes; add $12 for each AV program containing 3 or more tapes. We offer attractive quantity discounts for bulk purchases of individual titles; call for more information.

ORDER BY E-MAIL: Order 24 hours a day from anywhere in the world. Use either address:
To order: service@ppress.com
To view the online catalog and/or order: http://www.ppress.com/

QUANTITY DISCOUNTS: For information on quantity discounts, please contact our sales department.

INTERNATIONAL ORDERS: Write, phone, or fax for quote and indicate shipping method desired. For international callers, telephone number is 503-235-0600 and fax number is 503-235-0909. Prepayment in U.S. dollars must accompany your order (checks must be drawn on U.S. banks). When quote is returned with payment, your order will be shipped promptly by the method requested.

NOTE: *Prices are in U.S. dollars and are subject to change without notice.*

PRODUCTIVITY PRESS, DEPT. BK, P.O. BOX 13390, PORTLAND, OR 97213-0390
Telephone: 1-800-394-6868   Fax: 1-800-394-6286

CONTINUE YOUR LEARNING WITH IN-HOUSE TRAINING AND CONSULTING FROM PRODUCTIVITY, INC. CLIENT SERVICES GROUP

Consulting Services

For over a decade, an expansive client base continues to recommend Productivity's Consulting Services to colleagues eager to accelerate their improvement efforts. We have established a lasting improvement process with companies from various industries, including textiles, printing and packaging, chemicals, and heavy equipment.

Assignments vary from results-driven trainings on the tools of Lean Production, to broad total company conversion projects dealing with strategic intent through organization design/redesign. Tailoring our methodology to accommodate site-specific organizational and performance considerations is a real strength of Productivity's Consulting Services.

Educational Resources

Our products and services are leading-edge, and have been used by most every company in the Fortune 500 and beyond. Topics include: Quick Changeover, Visual Workplace, Lean Production Systems, Total Productive Maintenance, and Mistake-Proofing.

We offer the following opportunities to enhance your improvement efforts: National Conferences, Training Events, Plant Tours, Industrial Study Missions, Master Series Workshops, and Newsletters.

Call the Productivity, Inc. Client Services Group and learn how we can provide Consulting Services and Educational Resources customized to fit your changing needs.

Telephone: 1-800-966-5423 (U.S. only) or 1-203-846-3777
Fax: 1-203-846-6883